# Entrepreneurship and Industry 4.0

# Entrepreneurship and Industry 4.0:

## *Balancing Entrepreneurial Exploration and Exploitation*

By

Krishna Raj Bhandari

**Cambridge Scholars**
Publishing

Entrepreneurship and Industry 4.0:
Balancing Entrepreneurial Exploration and Exploitation

By Krishna Raj Bhandari

This book first published 2021

Cambridge Scholars Publishing

Lady Stephenson Library, Newcastle upon Tyne, NE6 2PA, UK

British Library Cataloguing in Publication Data
A catalogue record for this book is available from the British Library



ISBN (10): 1-5275-6972-1
ISBN (13): 978-1-5275-6972-0

# TABLE OF CONTENTS

# FOREWORD

The inequality narratives and the implications for capitalism, communism, and socialism, are the primary precursor of modern economics. However, Posner and Weyl (2018) still believe in markets to bring fairness and prosperity for all. The rationale behind this idea is not to abandon the free-market system but to think of new ways to organize markets for everyone's good. Though I appreciate the argument brought by the book, I argue that entrepreneurial exploration (e.g. innovation to solve social and environmental problems) and exploitation (reaping profits while keeping society and environment healthy and sustainable respectfully) might be a better approach. We assert that entrepreneurship and green-social entrepreneurship, usually called the Social Business Model, suggested by Nobel Laureate Professor Muhammad Yunus, may change at a pace that society can absorb. Even though 'Radical Markets' bring new hope for change and reconciliatory mechanisms for failing capitalism, to operationalize it and make it happen, societies must also have the absorptive capacity.

To build this absorptive capacity, one needs to start with the Social Business Model, but the goal may be to reach the Radical Markets-based mechanism. In the war against inequality, if I have been able to bring a slow but sustainable means to achieve equality for all, I am highly grateful for the society full of poverty, which triggered my thoughts to ask how we can eradicate inequality from the face of the earth. If we can work on this challenge, we may restore the individual dignity which has been destroyed by wars and conflicts around the world. If an individual is not at peace within himself, he will inflict death and sorrow on the world, and for himself. My assertion is to bring equal entrepreneurial opportunity and make it accessible to all. Having access itself does not make each successful; we need to make sure that schools and colleges need to build the entrepreneurial curriculum, implement it, and change the job-seekers' culture to that of job-creators; the latter must be celebrated in society as sportspeople are. Everyone is planning to emulate a hundred years of Silicon Valley's entrepreneurial success; however, it may become just a wish, unless and until, societies can build a culture of learning from failure as a norm, rather than an exception.

The entrepreneurial drive, and the culture to foster it, may seem friendly. Still, the pain points one has to reflect in hundreds of failures to understand new sutra for success has a proven process. It is becoming critical to revisit the same to bring about the changes triggered by new waves of industry 4.0 technologies. The earlier notions of Lean Startups, Customer Development, and Business Model Canvas need to be brought under the umbrella of March's (1991) idea of balancing exploration and exploitation for sustainable competitive advantage. Though the literature has captured this notion for large corporations, using a similar balancing act in entrepreneurial ventures is scant. This book answers many readers' requests to expand the book chapter I wrote a year ago with the title "Balancing Exploration and Exploitation Through the Customer Development Model: Leveraging Industry 4.0 for Sustainable Performance". The model and outline developed in this chapter have been extended to greater details in this book.

The time was ripe a year ago to think about the emerging wave, but the time is even better now, as Silicon Valley is emerging as a hub for long-term thinking with the Long-Term Stock Exchange brought about by Eric Ries and his colleagues. This gives hope for the entrepreneurs to think for sustainable businesses rather than rent-seeking parasites. However, we need to be skeptical in raising high hopes, as it takes time to change the entrepreneurial culture and discourse in society. As we have seen from Greta Thunberg's movement for climate change, and the call from Occupy Wall Street movements, the triggers for capitalism to correct its course have been emerging and gaining critical mass. I am hopeful I may see the vision of equality for all through democracy and capitalism — meaning through ballot, but not bullet. Yes, China's movement to eradicate poverty has been working, but it raises an eyebrow as to whether it will be sustainable. The equality syndrome was happening in the Soviet era also, but it crumbled in no time.

One may argue that the Soviet era was under a command economy, while China's President Xi's era is based on a free-market economy and controlled one-party rule. The Constitution of Liberty, written by Nobel Laureate Hayek, argues that suppression and surveillance may work with the less-educated population. When the essential human nature to be free and seek self-interest is suppressed for a long time, it may explode like a human bomb. I am sure China is awakening to this reality through Hong Kong's recent uprising, and building a slow-but-sure path to make liberty a choice in the end, when equality reigns over through the current model.

With the Bhandari Model, the goal is the same: equality for all, dignity for all, peace for all, and prosperity. However, in this model, the path to achieving this reality is based on a balancing act between entrepreneurial exploration and exploitation. The existing models of shareholder value maximization pursued by the firm have failed capitalism to some level — not because the model is inefficient, but the government's tax to provide equal opportunity to its citizens has been ineffective. The scalability needed to solve this crisis is not possible. Thus, enterprises tackling social and environmental problems and making a profit simultaneously would be a sustainable solution, as Grameen Bank demonstrated in Bangladesh, and worldwide.

Love, Peace, Prosperity

1st Feb 2021
Helsinki, Finland

## REFERENCE

Posner, E. A., & Weyl, E. G. (2018). *Radical markets: Uprooting capitalism and democracy for a just society*. Princeton University Press.

# CHAPTER 1

# INTRODUCTION


## ABSTRACT

*Industry 4.0 (i4.0) can unleash new business models or develop essential insights for a better decision-making process. The emergence of i4.0 not only unleashes technologies like IoT, AI, cloud computing, machine learning, robotics, and 5G, but also Big Data Analytics (BDA). It is enhancing entrepreneurial exploration and exploitation at its best for solving data challenges, process challenges, and management challenges. i4.0 can enhance value creation and value capture at the same time, with efficiency which is unmatched so far. First, balancing exploration and exploitation literature is reviewed to build an understanding of extant knowledge. Based on this review's research agenda, this book answers a key concern of how entrepreneurs can balance entrepreneurial exploration and exploitation in i4.0. The analytics world is moving beyond descriptive to predictive, and in the future, it will be more prescriptive, enabled by AI, machine learning, expert systems, and 5G. Thus, the future of entrepreneurial exploration and exploitation depends on how information is used to develop an insight into making intelligent, smart, and fact-based decision-making to take actions that may have real-time correction mechanisms and a new wave of quality, productivity, and customer intimacy.*



Keywords: Customer Development, Lean Startup, Industry 4.0, Quality Culture, Blue Ocean

## INTRODUCTION

Since the publication of "Balancing Exploration and Exploitation" (March 1991) to help understand the organizational learning from the lens of balancing exploration and exploitation, to the current review by Almahendra and Ambos (2015), the literature is mature enough in hailing the future changes triggered by i4.0. The concept of balancing exploration and exploitation has been studied in multiple ways with various definitions, new conceptualizations, measurements, and multiple forms of applying the idea to get its living course (Almahendra & Ambos 2015). The organizational issues and activities classified as exploration are search, variation, risk-taking, experimentation, play, flexibility, discovery, and innovation (March 1991, 71). Similarly, exploitation includes issues and activities such as refinement, choice, production, efficiency, selection, implementation, and execution (March 1991, 71). When problems and activities are search-oriented, and managers are allowed to take risks, conduct experiments, and invest in flexibility, discovery, and innovation, the organization positions itself as an innovative company. Similarly, when organizational issues and activities are thinking of refining a product or process, building multiple options in products and services, driven by an efficiency mantra with a relentless focus on execution as a capability, the organization positions itself as an efficiency-driven firm.

Literature in exploration and exploitation has volumes to speak about large corporations, and, at some level, SMEs, since the publication of a highly cited article by March (1991). The original idea even encouraged papers to study S&P 500 companies to understand their balancing act of exploration and exploitation orientation ((Uotila et al. 2009). The relationship between the exploration of the search for the business model, and the exploitation of existing organizational learning competencies, is a sound approach to understanding organizational success, as suggested by March (1991). Resource allocation challenges, such as the distribution of costs and benefits, are spread across different times and spaces for those searching and exploitation phases, and ecological interactions. The latter is even true in the new wave of i4.0. The move is from automation and efficiency to smart, intelligent products, connected in the cloud, and accessible for top management on a real-time basis.

March (1991) not only studied the mutual learning between members of an organization and an organizational code, but he also pioneered an idea on how learning leads to competitive advantage and competition for supremacy. This contribution's significance is that focusing on exploitation may be beneficial in the short-run, but self-destructive in the long-run (March 1991). However, in the new era of i4.0, the competitive supremacy or unfair advantage is inbuilt into the new business model, but this will be supported by competitive supremacy where collaboration across firm boundaries and functional boundaries is happening. Ecosystem thinking with new notions of platformization, servitization, and building smartness into products and services, will be the future.

The assertion that short-term myopia of the success trap must not be the reason for start-up failure by premature scaling, is one of the significant problems in start-ups. Having such good coverage of studies about the balancing act of exploration and exploitation in large corporations and SMEs does not help start-ups, as start-ups are not small-scale versions of large companies. There are institutions set up to explore new possibilities, such as new products, or to search for a business model under extreme uncertainty conditions (Ries 2011). While the existing literature is alien to the concept under discussion, the emerging i4.0 wave makes the topic even more interesting in understanding the implications of this new wave of technological change in entrepreneurial exploration and exploitation.

As the literature review for this work was done during the author's dissertation process, a long chapter on this area is avoided. Still, Bhandari (2017) is used as a reference to move forward. Similarly, this book is an extension of my earlier book chapter on the topic, which had high demand, and so the publisher wanted to build a comprehensive book on the same subject. Then, rather than being a vision-driven book, it was developed in a small, minimum viable, book chapter, to test the readers' feedback. Now we have a full text at the readers' service. This is precisely what a customer development model and lean start-up suggests. I revisited those concepts in the context of industry 4.0 and modification on a scale that demands a book in itself, as the balancing of entrepreneurial exploration and exploitation in i4.0. Where I have written the full book in the first phase, and the readers have not liked it, this follows the old paradigm of developing a product and figuring out the product-market fit afterwards. However, I have practiced the development process which I preached in the book itself. By demonstrating the product-market fit as an example, the book itself is an example of how to avoid start-up - or for that matter, any project - failure.

Failure in start-ups is the norm rather than an exception. However, the author's lean start-up approach gives a guideline, with optimization as a differentiation factor of the book in the BMOL loop, while testing the very early MVPs or MVDPs where the minimum viable product is desirable also. The old business model canvas becomes i4.0BMC, where unfair advantage, platformization, and innovation with sustainable development, are integrated. These notions will propel our mindset of curiosity and shaping future development to the next level.

## BACKGROUND

The new wave of Industry 4.0 (i4.0) makes many business models obsolete and may demand regeneration of the existing business models. While many authors have analyzed this change, the purpose of this book is to focus its impact on entrepreneurial exploration and exploitation. Though practitioners have been using multiple models such as the customer development model, lean start-up, or business model canvas (BMC), these models need to be aligned with the existing scientific literature on exploration and exploitation started by March (1991). While March (1991) proposed the model for general exploration and exploitation, this book focuses on the entrepreneurial exploration and exploitation triggered by the new wave of i4.0.

By linking the rigorous academic domain with the emerging practitioner's methods and tools, I have started to rectify the significant criticism faced by lean start-up methods of being experience-based rather than evidence-based. However, standalone evidence-based research to validate lean concepts is further due. The earlier wave of information technology triggered automation and efficiency. But the new surge of i4.0 puts pressure on the entrepreneur to adapt to this new reality, which changes the firms' value chains, and creates smart and intelligent products and services, real-time optimization of performance, and transparency and flatness in the hierarchy. Thus, it is timely to revisit existing business and management concepts where innovation has been costly so far. Perhaps a new dawn of successful creation is possible, due to real-time optimization algorithms.

A deep dive into the existing literature on exploration and exploitation is covered with an open mind as to what happens to the current models when i4.0 becomes a reality and passes the hype phase. Neither March's (1991) concept on exploration and exploitation, nor Blank's (2017) ideas on lean start-ups, customer development, and business model search, would be sufficient. Existing literature in the management domain hardly introduces a nuance variable of technological uncertainty into a firm's performance equation. Whenever Porter and Heppelman (2014, 2015) attempted to do so, a new wave of research in this domain emerged. In an attempt to grasp this reality, this book focuses on the impact of IoT, AI, machine learning, cloud computing, 5G, etc., on business performance.

## EXPLORATION AND EXPLOITATION AS AN ARTIFACT, AND ENTREPRENEURSHIP AS A CALLING

### Issues, Controversies, Problems

**Entrepreneurial Exploration and Exploitation: The Persevere or Pivot Decision.** The exploration-exploitation research has evolved into multiple directions since March's (1991) article on the topic. However, when i4.0 is in the emergent stage, understanding this change's fundamental nature from the lens of entrepreneurial exploration and exploitation needs attention from researchers. This is an attempt to explore how the forthcoming changes in technology will impact entrepreneurial exploration and exploitation. During my entrepreneurial investigation in multinational and start-up worlds alike, I encountered that most promising business ideas or start-up ideas fail at the point of either persevering or pivoting — meaning that when they need to pivot, companies scale it up. This resonates with the Startup Genome report (Marmer, Herrmann, Dogrultan, Berman, Eesley & Blank 2011). However, this book aims to decode this problem from the rigorous academic lens and bridge the theoretical lens and practitioners' experience. Thus, in this notion, exploration and exploitation are just an artifact, while entrepreneurship is a calling.

The underlying question now is to ask whether new waves of technologies will enable more mature scaling or not. Products and services are becoming smart and connected with the cloud, reshaping the value chain internally and changing the competitive game in parallel. The highest number of observations in the pivot or persevere stage in Figure 1 indicates that, most of the time, firms pass the gate without thinking whether the product-market fit is there or not. If we recall Moore (2002), it may be a false feeling that the customer we have at the customer validation stage will continue to market us throughout the product lifecycle. *Crossing the Chasm* (Moore 2002) is a grand challenge for any business if planning to scale the product or venture.

Around 32% of ventures scale prematurely. Another 18% fail in the customer validation process, and 17% of firms fail to build the company even if they have done well in the persevere phase. Similarly, 16% of firms fail due to the founder's attention span on vital strategic issues related to products, markets, and product-market fit, as shown in Figure 1. Only 10% of companies fail to create the customer, while only 7% of firms fail due to not figuring out the real customer in the early phase of idea generation. These percentages reveal a pattern that entrepreneurs are profitable in entrepreneurial exploration, but bad at entrepreneurial exploitation. Thus, a founder's team must balance these skills. Usually, finding an ambidextrous entrepreneur is very hard, but building an ambidextrous founding team is possible. From day one, the firm's focus must be on creating innovative products, but at the same time, they need to build a solid revenue pipeline so that the firm succeeds in taking off before it is too late; however, premature scaling is not an option.

The book by Moore (2002) called *Crossing the Chasm* was a classic in understanding how start-ups can progress from the stage of early adoption to mass-market customers. However, with the emergence of a new wave of new technology, products, business models, and machine intelligence, those existing models fall short, as suggested by Porter and Heppelman (2014, 2015). In earlier waves, automation and efficiency were the key drivers; collaboration with all partners, including customers, is needed in the new wave. Thus, the emergence of new cloud infrastructure will provide a massive new market for technology giants and start-ups alike.

**Culture of Fear vs. Trust and Empowerment**. The author of this book witnessed the colossal rise of Nokia, as an insider, and its turnaround as an outsider. Though multinational, Nokia has an entrepreneurial culture. Though it is not an excellent example for start-ups, we can learn lessons from the literature which elaborately discussed why Nokia failed in one wave of technology while succeeding in the next. Vuori and Huy (2016) argue that distributed attention and shared emotions are critical issues in the innovation process's success or failure. Lessons learned from such a narrative can be used in start-ups as well, but with caution, as start-ups are not small-scale versions of large corporations — whether we want to build a culture of trust and empowerment or fear. If you wish to place short-term focus on exploiting existing competencies, a culture of fear might work for a time, while pursuing a culture of exploration demands cultural DNA with trust and empowerment. Thus, start-ups need to figure out 'who' in the team first, rather than 'what.' Though 'culture eats strategy for breakfast', distributed attention is a real problem when resources are thin, and time to compete is short. Innovation cycles are faster than we thought, which drives temporal myopia. As listed below, balancing entrepreneurial exploration and exploitation requires balancing each subtopic under the exploration and exploitation umbrella. Success through innovation, search, differentiation, and experiment, must be balanced with success through efficiency and optimization.

**Balancing Entrepreneurial Exploration and Exploitation**

1. **Entrepreneurial Exploration:**
   a. Success through innovation,
   b. Search, differentiation,
   c. Experiment.
2. **Entrepreneurial Exploitation:**
   a. Success through efficiency,
   b. Optimization.

As shown in Figure 1, 32% of ventures fail at the pivot or persevere decision gate, as, most of the time, premature scaling becomes a bottleneck. Another 18% of failures are during the customer validation phase. This phase is critical, as minimum viable and desirable product (MVDP)-related assumptions, and hypotheses testing get it wrong. Another 17% of ventures fail in company development, 16% having the wrong attention from founders, 10% during the customer creation phase, and 7% during the customer discovery process. As shown in the Pareto map, it is critical to make proper scaling-up decisions, which is the most fundamental stage for start-up failures.

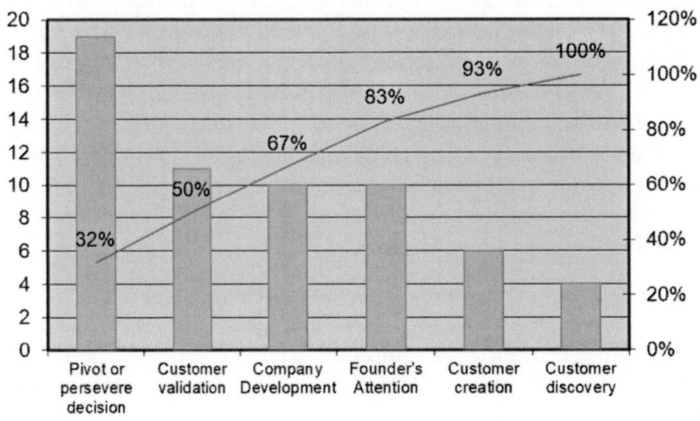


Figure 1-1. Pareto Map for Startup Failure (Based on Author's Observations)

The central idea of i4.0-related change is that, as the firm and industry boundaries are fading, and real-time optimization of performance is possible through live experiments and decision making, platformization will be the driving force in each industry, as is evident through the business model of Facebook, Apple, Alibaba, Netflix, and Google's (FAAANG's) approach. The exciting part is that manufacturing companies will embrace a new wave of servitization to build and bundle services with their product. This is possible due to digitalization, and the performance impact of such services would be high. Therefore, the future industrial landscape of i4.0 is more or less comprised of digital companies with a platform concept embedded into them, whether they are start-ups or large firms.

Large firms' research in balancing these exploration and exploitation-related activities and issues has been significant. However, the research in balancing the two delicate dilemmas in entrepreneurial ventures is scarce to my knowledge. This is fundamentally the reason for substantial start-up failures. They are in the 'failure-trap', as they are busy with exploration, and they are not good at exploitation at the right time. Even the strategic choices for entrepreneurial exploration and exploitation are challenging to solve, as the runway for start-up survival is usually too small compared to the large firm context, as the competition for scarce resource is very high. There is no room for too much or too little exploitation — rowing this boat with both hands is necessary to sail it to safe harbor amidst ever-changing reality. As stated in the definition, start-ups are ventures searching for a new business model in an environment which is too uncertain. Therefore, we cannot rely on the school of planning knowledge when we need the school of tools and expertise for experimentation and learning. I know, the Porterian school of thought is not happy with my claim in the previous sentence, but Mintzberg may be smiling on the other side, and he believes in the emergent nature of strategy. Similarly, now for the first time, Sarasvathy's (2001) effectuation logic gets recognition by the author's attempt to tell the world that lean start-up is not a brand-new concept, as it is rooted in effectuation logic in greater detail.

## SOLUTIONS AND RECOMMENDATIONS

Balancing entrepreneurial exploration and exploitation demands the understanding of exploration-related risks and exploitation-related risks. I use risk and uncertainty as mostly synonymous for simplification purposes, but the concept is more in assessing the uncertainty. First, an example of exploration-related risks may be not identifying the real needs for the product or service we are developing. The entrepreneurial quest is not an easy task. We are searching for new business models — to build a new business line, turn around the existing business for large corporations, and test the new business model for start-ups. In both cases, proper assessment of entrepreneurial risk is a significant factor, as shown in Table 1. In the quest for early profitability, less focus on R&D and premature scaling may happen to drag the start-up into exploitation or a profit trap. These traps are natural when time and resources are enemies, and there is no knowledge in the team or so-called board on the timing of scaling up. Even seasoned venture capitalists (VCs) will face this dilemma in start-ups working in the i4.0 domain, as knowing or simulating the venture's hockey stick growth is still a challenge. However, we will have more real-data possibilities based on experiments and simulations given by the BMOL loop in the i4.0BMC validation phase.

Having everything change in an entrepreneur's favor makes the future of entrepreneurship a good calling, while entrepreneurial exploration and exploitation become an artifact. However, usually, entrepreneurs are exploration oriented — they are good at innovating but bad in monetization. They are mesmerized by their innovation, but the growth potential does not lure them. Nevertheless, understanding exploration myopia and sailing the firm further along the exploitation curve early enough, but at the right time, are critical decision challenges for any entrepreneur. A sense of urgency is needed, as speed may be the only competitive advantage, but deciding in a hurry and repenting in free time should not happen. The entrepreneurial quest and mindset, geared towards unleashing the potential of new growth and seeing humanity free from poverty and climatic disasters, must give an entrepreneur a mission that keeps me awake during the night to seek solutions to these perplexing problems. However, never in human civilization, has such a mass flourishing of innovation existed with such a vibrant innovation ecosystem. Now is the time for many to pursue this vocation. Entrepreneurship-related degree programs and entrepreneur-in-residence concepts must exist in all types of companies. The future is bright, not only for exploring but also for exploitation, not only for small companies with global ambitions but also for large companies.

In the horizontal axis in Figure 2, the likelihood of risk is plotted, while the vertical axis represents the level of risk associated with entrepreneurial exploration. The size of the ball in the diagram indicates the level of risk. The larger the size, the more planning to mitigate the same risk is crucial. In our example, risk one is called need assessment, and bet two is called a new business model search; two major risk factors with a high chance of happening. Therefore, our resources to mitigate the same must be allocated from early on. As discussed in the introduction, issues, and problems sections, literature gives prescriptions for entrepreneurial exploration and exploitation. Still, there is a gap in the literature on how to achieve this elusive balance. Therefore, our example tools and tables with illustrative graphs drive the discussion on 'how' a balance of entrepreneurial exploration and exploitation could be achieved. However, in doing so, we are focusing only on the industry 4.0 (i4.0)-related activities and processes, starting with the existing models suggested by Ries (2010) and Blank (2013) to build a modified model to embrace the change initiated by i4.0.

**Table 1-1 Entrepreneurial exploration-related example activities and their risk assessment**

| **Process Name:** | Entrepreneurial exploration | **Process Owner:** | Dr. Krishna Raj Bhandari | |
|---|---|---|---|---|
| | | **Date:** | 12/09/2019 | |
| | | | | |
| **Risk Identification** | | **Risk Analysis** | | |
| **Risk#** | **Description** | **Likelihood** | **Consequences** | **Risk Level** |
| 1 | Need assessment | 4.50 | 4.00 | 8.5 |
| 2 | New business model search | 3.50 | 4.25 | 7.75 |
| 3 | New business model validation | 4.00 | 3.00 | 7 |
| 4 | Less focus on R&D | 3.00 | 3.00 | 6 |
| 5 | Exploitation or profit trap | 2.50 | 2.50 | 5 |

In this pursuit of modifications, or rather of an alignment, my attempt has been to link these practitioners' contributions with March (1991) and Sarasvathy (2001). They gave us the exploration and exploitation lens and the effectuation lens, respectively. By linking these theories with that of lean start-ups, a comprehensive understanding may be developed. Dwelling on the linkages and building decision models, however, will be done in later chapters. Figure 1 raises the alarm to entrepreneurs to avoid the failure trap, or the relentless search trap, by using a minimum viable product or service concept in validating customer needs and testing i4.0BMCs.

Taking this adventure as a potential contribution to reducing the start-up failure rate, I found my calling. Sleepless nights of digesting various concepts and models to synthesize into more comprehensive thinking have given me a rewarding feeling. However, if an entrepreneur takes it as a simplified view of the complex world, I may take it as fair criticism. Nevertheless, the attempt here is to clarify many issues about the impact of i4.0 itself that might perplex entrepreneurs and academicians alike. There is a lack of understanding of this phenomenon, as universities have not yet started to train the future workforce, nor have best practices on this front emerged. Therefore, sandwiched between these dilemmas, this book seeks to find its space.

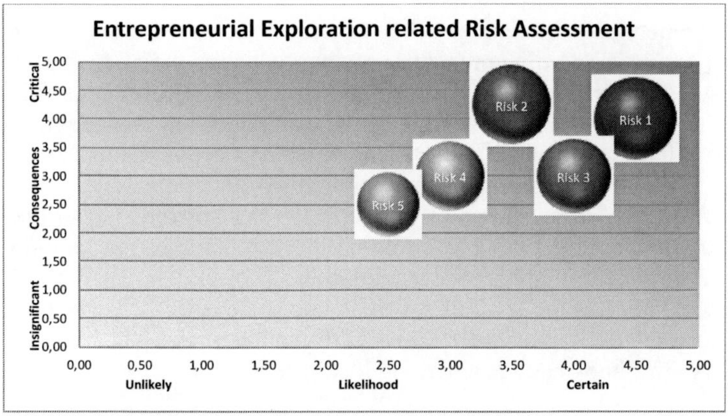


Figure 1-2. Risk assessment in entrepreneurial exploration

As we have seen in the exploration-related dilemma in the previous section, this section discusses the significant dimensions of entrepreneurial exploitation-related risks, which can be listed as corporate arrogance (or founders' arrogance), the CEOs' (founders') attention to the right issues, the challenges of a saturated market, the profit (or exploitation) trap, and agency problems associated with the CEOs' benefit maximization at the expense of shareholders, as shown in Table 2. These factors are symbolic but demand proper understanding.

**Table 1-2. Entrepreneurial exploitation and risk assessment**

| | | | | |
|---|---|---|---|---|
| **Process Name:** | Entrepreneurial exploitation | **Process Owner:** | Dr. Krishna Raj Bhandari | |
| | | **Date:** | 12-09-19 | |
| **Risk Identification** | | **Risk Analysis** | | |
| **Risk#** | **Description** | **Likelihood** | **Consequences** | **Risk Level** |
| 1 | Corporate arrogance | 4.50 | 4.00 | 8.5 |
| 2 | CEO's attention problem | 3.50 | 4.25 | 7.75 |
| 3 | Market saturation | 4.00 | 3.00 | 7 |
| 4 | Profit (exploitation) trap | 3.00 | 3.00 | 6 |
| 5 | Agency problem | 2.50 | 2.50 | 5 |

Entrepreneurial exploitation is not an easy task either. This demands a sharp focus on avoiding premature scaling, which is the primary factor in start-up failures, as per the start-up genomes report. We discuss efficiency, cost leadership, and optimization, of the existing business model for large corporations, and explore and implement the new business model for start-ups. In both cases, proper assessment of entrepreneurial risk is a significant factor, as shown in Figure 3. On the horizontal axis, one can plot the likelihood of trouble, while on the vertical axis, one can plot the dimensions of entrepreneurial exploration. The size of the balls in the diagram indicates the level of risk. The larger the size, the better planning to mitigate the same risk is crucial. Mitigating such risks becomes the focus of this book and the emerging literature on i4.0.

Key dimensions that entrepreneurs or entrepreneurial managers need to focus on to balance the entrepreneurial exploration and exploitation are listed, for example as in Table 3: balancing search and profitability, balancing effectiveness and efficiency, balancing CEO's attention for short-term and long-term thinking, balancing agency problems with shareholder's interest, and focusing on sustainable development. Once the proper risk assessment is accomplished for both entrepreneurial exploration and exploitation processes, founders or entrepreneurial managers need to consider balancing them both, as shown in Figure 4. Risks 1 and 2 are substantial in size compared to others, revealing the level of risk and attention needed to solve the same. Such a map gives an idea of optimizing the resources required for each phase of the customer development model embedded in lean start-up (Blank 2013).

Balancing the twin trade-offs of exploration and exploitation was implicit, or not dealt with, in extant literature. The illustrations are just an example, and the content in tables in assessing the risk and implied uncertainty will be entirely different for different start-ups.

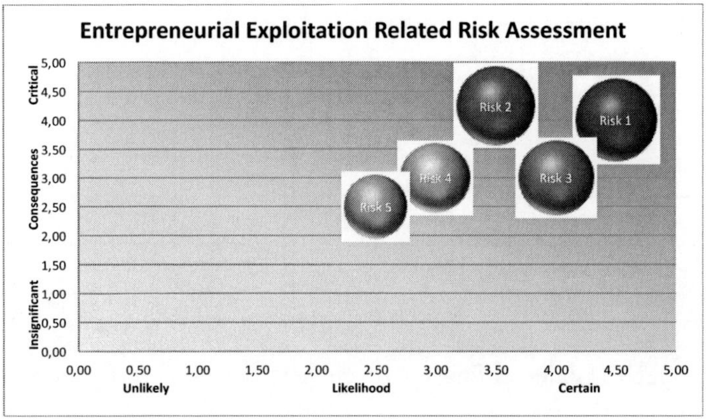


Figure 1-3. Assessment of risk in entrepreneurial exploitation

As illustrated above, the extant literature suggests that existing entrepreneurship models fall short in understanding the emerging nature of i4.0 related changes. We need models that adapt to the changing process itself, and preplanned approaches do not hold in a dynamic industry. Sarasvathy (2001) outlined how opportunity creation is possible by focusing on who you are, what you know, and who you know. The emergent nature of means orientation, though with a vision, brings feedback loops in learning and adaptation, as and when the change unfolds. Management discipline is more focused on goal-orientation but having a means-orientation mindset is beneficial in uncertain environments such as triggered by i4.0. Practitioners have used the customer development model, lean start-up, and business model canvas, to understand the existing entrepreneurship development processes.

**Table 1-3. Risk identification in balancing entrepreneurial exploration and exploitation**

| | | | |
|---|---|---|---|
| **Process Name:** | Balancing entrepreneurial exploration and exploitation | **Process Owner:** | Dr. Krishna Raj Bhandari |
| | | **Date:** | 12-09-19 |

| **Exploration Related Risk Identification** | | **Risk Analysis** | | |
|---|---|---|---|---|
| **Risk#** | **Description** | **Likelihood** | **Consequences** | **Risk Level** |
| 1 | Balancing search and profitability | 4.50 | 4.00 | 8.5 |
| 2 | Balancing effectiveness and efficiency | 3.50 | 4.25 | 7.75 |
| 3 | Balancing CEO's attention in short-term and long-term focus | 4.00 | 3.00 | 7 |
| 4 | Balancing agency problem with shareholder's interest | 3.00 | 3.00 | 6 |
| 5 | Focusing on sustainable development | 2.50 | 2.50 | 5 |

The research frontier calling for researchers is still in its infancy. A new innovative business model, efficiency projects, and implications for theory and research of management are on the verge of emergence. We need to understand the relationships between business model alternatives, competitive strategy, and the resulting performance outcomes, in the new industrial internet wave. The changes suggested by Burmeister et al. (2016) have some exciting implications for managements' theory and practice. The new wave offers the possibility for customization of products and services and efficiency optimization at the same time. This will give an edge for those who understand the meaning of adaptation to the individual customer needs. Figure 4 demonstrates how one can assess the balancing acts and plan for mitigation of the same. In doing such an assessment, the alert mechanism in collecting the right information enabled by i4.0 technologies must be thought through to avoid start-up failure, which is a blessing in disguise. I am hopeful my assertion will be valid. Still, one looming danger is the emergence of machines faster than human intelligence and reaching singularity faster than was at first thought. Human civilization falls into machines' hands when our intelligence becomes a witness to machine control of human civilization. We become prisoners of our creation. I trust the opposite would come true, but the fear of the unknown drives us insane sometimes.

Porter's idea of competitive supremacy based on either cost leadership or differentiation is no more valid. The new change wave will delete the concept of 'stuck-in-the-middle' syndrome while pursuing both cost leadership and differentiation. The old idea of 'red ocean'-based cut-throat competition is no more valid, while the new 'blue ocean' thinking, where competition is irrelevant, is becoming a reality. As business level thinking is changing, so does functional level thinking — balancing the trade-off between novelty-centricity and efficiency-centricity (Zott & Amit 2007) in business model design is becoming a reality illustrated by multiple cases (Burmeister et al. 2016). Thus, both entrepreneurial exploration and exploitation are possible at the same time.

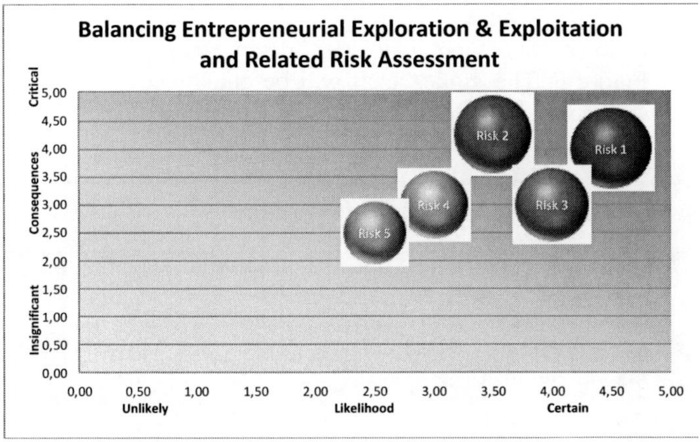


Figure 1-4. Risk map in balancing entrepreneurial exploration and exploitation

In projects, there is a concept of piloting the small scale. Still, it does not have a similar philosophy to the build-measure-optimize-learn (BMOL) loop enabled by hypothesis testing of industry 4.0 Business Model Canvas (i4.BMC). Thus, based on my approach to balancing both exploration and exploitation in the innovation process, existing literature has just scratched the surface in Bhandari (2017). Figure 5 summarizes the proposition made by Bhandari's (2018) framework by synthesizing the customer development model, BM*O*L, and entrepreneurial exploration and exploitation. This will be revisited in Chapter 3 under the theoretical framework later.

From Blank (2005) to Klotz (2020), there is a critical shift in Blank's thinking. In the age of 'epiphany' (Blank 2005), the idea was to work with budding young entrepreneurs where the experience was not that important, or the learning loops of lean start-ups. But Klotz's (2020) interview with Blank suggested that when the 'experiential learning' of scientists and engineers is combined with lean launchpad concepts, the venture becomes strong, and able to thrive in chaos and uncertainty, as shown in Figure 5. The BM*O*L loop curves depict the difference between an inexperienced team and an experienced team. In this notion, all phases of customer development benefit from faster execution, but are learning-focused. This makes experiential learning a powerful tool for entrepreneurial ventures themselves.

Stanford gave the world Blank's and Ries' lean start-up and customer development models. On the other hand, Harvard presented a theory called 'jobs-to-be-done by the customer with the product or service we are offering them' (Christensen, Hall, Dillon, & Duncan, 2016). The latter becomes an integrating theoretical lens in the comprehensive model, as shown in Figure 5. The model itself will be elaborated in Chapter 3, but the framework's building blocks are shown in this chapter.

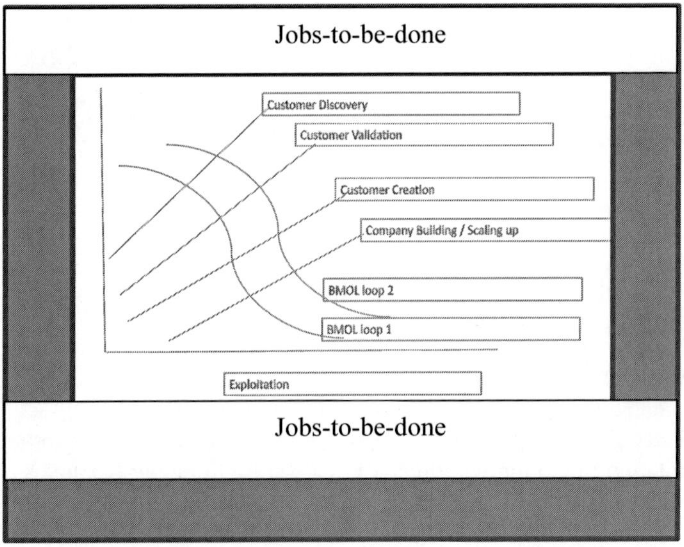


Figure 5. Author's synthesis of jobs-to-be-done theory, customer development model, lean start-up, and balancing exploration and exploitation

The lean start-up method suggested that the build-measure-learn (BML) loop must be executed relentlessly to search for a new business model. However, in the i4.0 era, the BM*O*L loop (Figure 6) is needed as optimization algorithms are most important in each development and company building cycle. This learning loop could be called an experiential learning loop (Klotz 2020); however, this learning may also be accumulated through scientific knowledge over the years of a career.

The i4.0 business model canvas (i4.0BMC) will also be developed in later chapters as a tool to implement the models suggested in Figures 5 and 6. These models are only good for the starting phase of the open innovation and platformization, which in itself gets modified, as and when feedback emerges from the system as it evolves. Thus, these models are organic, and will become new wisdom from entrepreneurial exploration and exploitation, as the context is different. The ecosystem will be diverse, the country of operation will be different, and its specific advantages will be distinct. However, customization is a real benefit when one can cater unique products and services to every individual customer in the age of i4.0. Pitfalls may be there, but the benefits provided by the new era will be many. We are at the cusp of a dawn of a new age full of surprises, and AI as new electricity may mean a future of fully self-learning machines and tools that makes repetitive tasks things of the past very soon. The future generation may just need to learn how to be creative, rather than memorizing any subject.

As discussed in the context of the larger framework, the BMOL loop also gets its guiding theory finally to solve the jobs-to-be-done by the customers or various use cases and storyboards related to scenario testing. In this core process, in earlier notions, more correlational attributes were collected. Still, now with Christensen et al.'s (2016) approach, a causal link between the product or service and the customer's buying behavior is identified. This tool gives a strong foundation where *Competing Against Luck* (Hall, Christensen, Dillon, & Duncan 2016) becomes finally feasible. According to the authors, it is more about understanding customers' choice and their behavior in making purchase decisions. This removes correlation in the process and builds causality in the real sense.

While executing learning loops based on hypothesis or minimum viable product (MVP), thinking beyond cost or revenue drivers and trying to think simultaneously about how to lower costs and increase revenue would be a plausible approach. However, in such phrases, the unit of progress is just the learning, which is also validated learning. These validated learning loops may change to persevere or pivot loops after customer validation. As we learn fast and fail-safe, this approach downplays the old planning school which was building a plan for an extended period and realizing the rejection from the first customer touchpoint. Such a system was a luxury of the past, and no one is investing in this paradigm and entrepreneurs' vision only. Yes, vision matters, but learning loops anchored on vision are even more critical. In an interview published by Klotz (2020), the father of the customer development model, S. Blank, admitted that "GE management wanted to train everybody to become innovators, rather than ensure that leaders understood where [innovation] in the company was, and how they could rapidly deploy new products and services. To expect everybody in a company to be an innovator was a mistake".

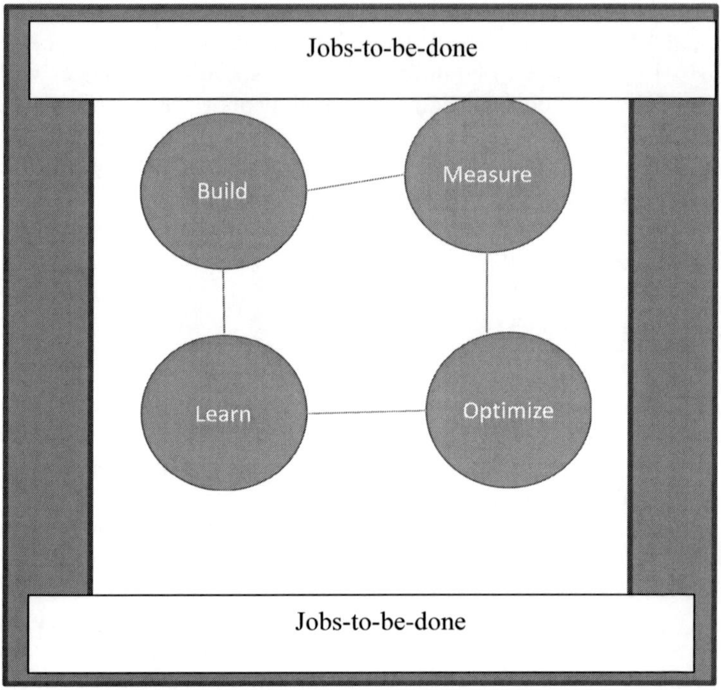


Figure 1-6. BMOL loop proposed by author by emphasizing 'optimize' and 'experiential learning' in i4.0 age

Thus, caution is needed in applying these concepts in large companies, and large companies are not the large scale of small companies. Many variables are known to the CEO and managers in large companies, such as customer needs, business models, customer segments, pricing, and even the customer's business model if the parent company is a B2B company. However, start-ups make assumptions to figure out all of those parameters unknown to the company. We need to understand the customer, build a new business model, figure out customer segments, develop new pricing structures, etc. As we do not know many issues, we search for a start-up rather than operating in large companies' execution mode. Therefore, without understanding these limitations and differences, applying tools from one domain to another, or vice versa, is a prescription for failure.

In the past, all the tools used in the start-up world were based on the planning school of management, which was developed in the context of large MNCs. In this way, entrepreneurs thought that start-ups are the small-scale versions of large MNCs. By applying the tools and methods used in large companies where most of the critical issues are known already, start-ups were failing at a larger scale. When this assumption and the same application were challenged recently, a new wave to prove the latest tools and techniques was underway but validating the same empirically has not been possible yet.

A new frontier emerging due to i4.0 needs to embrace a reality that all external factors in a business environment will be fundamentally different, as shown in Figure 7. Suppose we assess the external environment through PESTLEG (Politics, Economics, Society, Technology, Environment, Law, and Global forces). In that case, humans have to make many difficult choices when the new era takes hold. For example, there will be a considerable debate on war or peace, layoffs or growth, hell or heaven, the collapse of society due to technology or control, pollution or renewables, and deadlock in legal systems or innovation to embrace the reality. Above all, global forces are either racing with the machine or against the machine. In designing any future business model, these trends must be assessed in greater detail (Kaplan & Haenlein 2020).

While doing PESTLE analysis, thoughts must be focused on understanding the implications of the same on the start-up, the environment, and society. The earlier notion of maximizing only shareholders' value or, for that matter, profit, is not sufficient, as the environmental degradation and social inequality have put planet earth at the edge of mass extinction. Perhaps the new wave of technologies will support entrepreneurs in executing the i4.0BMC (detailed discussion in Chapter 3) so that the future becomes a safe place to live and leave a legacy to our children and future generations.

As the external environment will be under transformation itself, the impact on businesses' internal environment will be more considerable than we assessed. As economics is associated with politics, sociology, and legal environment, studying a firm under situations where all of these three forces are under uncertainty, a start-up in the i4.0 era will be vulnerable, but at the same time, if an entrepreneur can turn the VUCA world into reaping the benefits of no regulation in early-stage this might become an opportunity as well. When regulators wake up and tighten the rules, a particular investment level has been returned by the income itself.

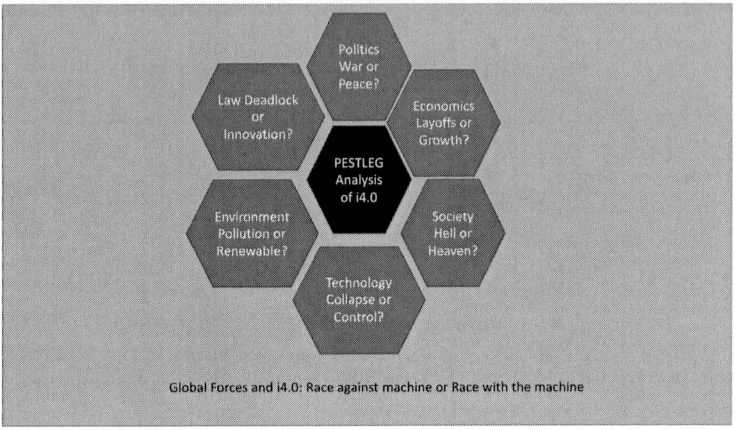


Figure 1-7. PESTLE and i4.0 (extended from AI to i4.0 from Kaplan and Haenlein (2020)).

## CONCLUSION

March (1991) argued for balancing exploration and exploitation, but there has been an uneasy vacuum linking this seminal work in the start-up world. I have attempted to fulfill this gap. The emergence of a new wave of technologies and the challenging climate risk makes one vulnerable to the emerging future. Not only assessing the risk, but also planning for the mitigation of the risks identified, would be a logical expansion of these frameworks. Though the book is designed for start-ups, it may be equally applicable to other sizes of firms, and it has been tested in large corporations — but with dismal success in the case of GE. However, there are many limitations to this work, as follows. First, though the models and narratives could be applied to different firms' sizes, one must be cautious in adopting the dimensions appropriate for a start-up or SME, or a multinational. Second, I may be biased in academic rigor compared to practical relevance, but this is where the gap lies. Most of the start-up literature is practitioner biased. Third, quantitative research to test the framework developed in this book is highly recommended, as the book project's scope and size does not allow me to do the same.

The impact of individual technology components of i4.0 on i4.0 BMC is a new research domain that demands my attention, and many others may contribute on the same side. As this book's scope is not to focus on individual technologies, but overall assessment, I may be blamed for too many generalizations. However, to develop the field further, someone needs to take blame and credit at the same time.

Thus, proper assessment of how to balance entrepreneurial exploration and exploitation-related risks is the first starting point to search for a new business model. The comprehensive framework combined with the customer development model, business model canvas, lean start-up, and entrepreneurial exploration and exploitation in Figures 5 and 6, will guide frameworks throughout the book, as discussed in detail in Chapter 3. Though the slight movement was initiated in start-ups, while implementing in large corporations, Blank cautions the entrepreneurial managers to be vigilant that it does not only become a discrete activity among hundreds. The real need is an "end-to-end innovation process" (Klotz 2020) that covers everything from buying, warehousing, curation, prioritization, and solution development to incubation to customer interaction. "That pipeline needs to be part of an overall innovation doctrine". Perhaps we are in the right time of human civilization to build that pipeline, and to implement an innovation doctrine which sweeps power, brings mega returns, builds sustainable societies, and respects the planet's fragile ecology while building entrepreneurial ecosystems where platformization is the new norm rather than the exception. Let us wake up the platform economy where double-sided markets make such platforms interesting for economists and practitioners alike. Juxta-positioning these domains would be an exciting task, and I am up for the challenge, as and when it unfolds.

## REFERENCES

Almahendra, R., & Ambos, B. (2015). Exploration and exploitation: a 20-year review of evolution and reconceptualization. *International Journal of Innovation Management*, *19*(01), 1550008.

Bhandari, K. R. (2018). Balancing Exploration and Exploitation Through Customer Development Model: Leveraging Industry 4.0 for Sustainable Performance. In *Analyzing the Impacts of Industry 4.0 in Modern Business Environments* (pp. 147-160). IGI Global.

Blank, S. (2017). Why the lean start-up changes everything? *Harvard Business Review*.

Burmeister, C., Lüttgens, D., & Piller, F. T. (2016). Business model innovation for Industrie 4.0: why the "Industrial Internet" mandates a new perspective on innovation. *Die Unternehmung*, *70*(2), 124-152.

Christensen, C. M., Hall, T., Dillon, K., & Duncan, D. S. (2016). Know your customers' jobs to be done. *Harvard Business Review*, *94*(9), 54-62.

Hall, T., Christensen, C., Dillon, K., & Duncan, D. (2016). Competing Against Luck: The Story of Innovation and Customer Choice. *EUA: HarperBusiness*.

Kaplan, A., & Haenlein, M. (2020). Rulers of the world, unite! The challenges and opportunities of artificial intelligence. *Business Horizons*, *63*(1), 37-50.

Marmer, M., Herrmann, B. L., Dogrultan, E., Berman, R., Eesley, C., & Blank, S. (2011). Start-up genome report extra: Premature scaling. *Start-up Genome*, *10*, 1-56.

March, J. G. (1991). Exploration and exploitation in organizational learning. *Organization Science*, *2*(1), 71-87.

Moore, G. A. (2007). Dealing with Darwin: How great companies innovate at every phase of their evolution. *Strategic Direction*, *23*(9).

Moore, G. A. (2002). Crossing the Chasm, revised edition. *New York: HarperBusiness Essentials*.

Porter, M. E., & Heppelmann, J. E. (2015). How smart, connected products are transforming companies. *Harvard Business Review*, *93*(10), 96-114.

Porter, M. E., & Heppelmann, J. E. (2014). How smart, connected products are transforming competition. *Harvard Business Review*, *92*(11), 64-88.

Klotz, F. (2020). Why Large Companies Struggle with Lean. *MIT Sloan Management Review*, *61*(2), 1-4.

Ries, E. (2011). *The lean start-up: How today's entrepreneurs use continuous innovation to create radically successful businesses*. Crown Books.

Vuori, T. O., & Huy, Q. N. (2016). Distributed attention and shared emotions in the innovation process: How Nokia lost the smartphone battle. *Administrative Science Quarterly*, *61*(1), 9-51.

## KEY TERMS AND DEFINITIONS

**Industry 4.0:** A new industrial wave generated due to the collective technologies such as 5G, cloud computing, machine learning, artificial intelligence, and internet of things (IoT), etc.

**Ethnocentric:** A belief that one's own culture is superior to other cultures. The abbreviation frequently used is i4.0.

**Customer Development Model:** The process of entrepreneurial innovation has been divided into four phases by Blank (2013): customer discovery, customer validation, customer creation, and company building

**BMOL Loop:** The original conceptualization based on the lean start-up method (Ries, 2011) of build, measure, and learn loop is augmented with 'optimize' by Bhandari (2018).

**Entrepreneurial exploration:** The process of innovation, search, explore and build new products or services.

**Entrepreneurial exploitation:** It is the process of efficiency, automation, and optimization of existing products or services or the early phase of new products or services.

# CHAPTER 2

# BALANCING EXPLORATION AND EXPLOITATION AND INDUSTRY 4.0

**ABSTRACT**

*Building a culture of innovation and quality from inception is the real mantra of success. In the earlier conceptualization of customer development model and lean start-up, or business model canvas, balancing entrepreneurial exploration and exploitation is not explicit, and culture does not take center stage in those models. Minimum viable products (MVP) were interpreted as quality-compromised products, in order to conduct customer discovery and customer validation. Also, in the age of industry 4.0, these existing models need to be adapted or modified to cater to changing reality. This chapter outlines the emerging change and the need for an adapted model(s). Though building product differentiation becomes the core of entrepreneurial exploration, creating cost savings through entrepreneurial exploitation must not be abandoned. The Blue Ocean Strategy emerges if balancing both value and cost trade-off is realized.*

Keywords: Entrepreneurial exploration, Entrepreneurial exploitation, Blue ocean strategy

## INTRODUCTION

In *Post Capitalism* (2016) Paul Mason raises an eyebrow at the proliferation of parallel currencies, time banks, cooperatives, and self-managed spaces. Rajan and Zingales (2004) are concerned about the challenges created by self-serving capitalists misusing the tenets of the free-market system. The beginning of a new era will be essential, as the outcry from academics to save capitalism from the capitalist will be possible just because of i4.0 wave technologies (Rajan and Zingales 2004). As civilization has tested multiple ways of organizing in society, the free market economy is the best fit for human society, which has an independent will and is governed by self-interest and God's invisible hand, as suggested by Adam Smith, the father of economics. However, laissez-faire capitalism is not an answer, nor a command economy, in the long run. Thus, the government's enabling role is a must by promoting the private sector and making it accountable for social cause and environmental damage.

Focusing only on profit or shareholder value maximization may not be the real mantra in the age of i4.0. This generation's capitalist dilemma is that the government is elected mainly by the private sector's lobbyists' donations and support. The private sector wants return on investments made to politicians and regulatory or other changes which will benefit the private sector operators and allow them to earn abnormal profits and compensation for their top management, especially CEOs. The corporates are powerful already, and the possibility of Schumpeterian creative destruction of existing business models is not possible, as regulations do not support innovation and disruption. By monopolizing the political system and, for that matter, the markets they are operating in, multinationals have more or less captured the notion of monopoly creation, or max duopoly creation in platform business or other similar businesses. In this scenario, the private sector is leveraging the power of vested politicians to safeguard its benefits through regulation that is beneficial to existing products and solutions, at the expense of Schumpeterian creative destruction to innovate and serve the society better.

As the new imperative of i4.0 is real-time optimization and control where data becomes the new oil, balancing both trade-offs/entrepreneurial exploration and exploitation is possible for the first time. However, one needs to build a culture of innovation and quality through inception. lean manufacturing systems are no longer part and parcel of manufacturing or established firms. Entrepreneurial ventures can grasp similar benefits through lean start-up and the BMOL loop, as discussed earlier. Nor have we abandoned the customer development model suggested by Blank (2005). This book is a focused approach to cater to the growing needs of i4.0 and the innovation and platformization it is enabling in each industry. The firm boundary is no more the locus of innovation and collaboration, nor is the industry boundary restricted. Thus, there is massive potential in embracing this new challenge to harness the entrepreneurial dynamism (Phelps 2013) in a real sense envisioned in true capitalism.

The i4.0 is a new beginning of an era that restores individual dignity, anchored in individual peace. After that, to the whole society where prosperity is the real success mantra, we need to understand the current certainties and utilize them in exploring new possibilities. In this pursuit of balancing the profit and search for innovation, an entrepreneur must be alert to a new emergent reality. The planning school that existed for the management of the last century will not rescue the entrepreneurial managers or the entrepreneurs themselves. They need Mintzberg's emergent view as a basis of strategy while experimentation and observation with optimization tools become a new reality. No situation is similar to the past, and the change itself is unique; as the transformation unfolds, it unfolds a new truth. Entrepreneurs are embracing the unknowns in large numbers now. All assumptions in i4.0BMC must be tested, retested, and understood, before jumping to conclusions of any sort.

## BACKGROUND

As election systems become corrupt, serving the multinationals' interest, conscious citizens must rise to build a fairer society with a healthy civil society or plural sector, so that neither the multinationals nor the government has high bargaining power in their pockets. Thus, Mintzberg suggests that a vibrant civil society is as essential as the entrepreneurial dynamism protected by innovation, IPR, and competition laws. With the advent of smart, interconnected products, with the possibility of real-time data for taking actions and decisions, professionals, people (consumers), the press, and the plural sector (civil society) (4Ps) alike can do the checks and balances of election expenses, make politicians accountable, and make the private sector socially responsible and environmentally friendly. The force of the 4Ps prevents the private interests trying to influence free markets' efficient function to serve their narrow interests and increases the level of economic opportunity in society (Rajan and Zingales 2004).

Whether in Silicon Valley or in a Wall Street company, the role of the entrepreneur and corporate entrepreneurship is becoming indispensable, as i4.0 will make large corporations vulnerable and force them to rethink their business model. In either approach, the only mantra of shareholders is that value maximization does not take hold, or traditional accounting-based measures of success are utilized. In this utopia called i4.0, enabling innovation and entrepreneurship, the customer lifetime value (CLV) becomes a guiding dependent or an outcome variable during the business model search phase towards scaling the company. This book is optimized with CLV, but the further research section later will delve into the potential for other variables such as social impact and environmental impact. However, these are implicit now in i4.0 Business Model Canvas (i4.0BMC). As briefly outlined in Chapter 1, the Conclusion and Further Research sections, we rely on CLV in this book, but the alertness of SDGs has not been sidelined. They are, in a sense, an outcome of pursuing CLV. However, measuring the impact in social and environmental benefit terms could be rewarding as well. This and other issues will be assessed in detail in the further research section here in this chapter, and in the full chapter dedicated to further research at the end.

## SIMULTANEOUS PURSUIT OF EXPLORATION AND EXPLOITATION

### Issues, Controversies, Problems

Industry 4.0 can unleash new business models or develop essential insights for a better decision-making process. It includes IoT, AI, cloud computing, machine learning, robotics, 5G, blockchain, and Big Data Analytics (BDA), which is enhancing entrepreneurial exploration and exploitation at its best to solve data, process, and management challenges. The i4.0 can enhance value creation and value capture at the same time with efficiency unmatched so far. Based on the literature review's research agenda, this book answers a key concern as to how entrepreneurs can balance entrepreneurial exploration and exploitation in i4.0 enabled innovation and platformization. The analytics world is moving beyond descriptive to predictive, and in the future, it will be more prescriptive enabled by AI, machine learning, expert systems, and 5G. Thus, the future of entrepreneurial exploration and exploitation depends on how information is used to develop an insight to make intelligent, smart, and fact-based decision-making to take actions that may have a real-time correction mechanism, and a new wave of quality, productivity, and customer satisfaction, is a reality.

As an example of technology's potential to make a fundamental change in economics and business as we know it so far, Rajan (2015) solely focused on changes due to technology in the 19th century. What the telegraph did for the history of capitalism, i4.0-based technologies as a bundle will do for 21st century capitalism, or a new way of organizing will advent the pervasive use of open innovation and platformization. Mass flourishing and entrepreneurial dynamism (Phelps 2013) will become a new reality if entrepreneurs can rescue capitalism from the existing capitalists themselves. Anthropologists focused on shaping a story that focused on primitive religion to accept scientific rationalism during the time of the telegraph. This struggle between sacred economics and scientific rationalism in 19th century Britain may repeat once again, as we are swept by the fear of being irrelevant when the skills needed for this century are not yet conceptualized. The value systems required to embrace the nearing fear of singularity makes one vulnerable. Rajan (2015) provides a potential narrative of how this could unfold. As and when some innovations will cover the planet in solving the current challenges of climate change, social inequality, income inequality, and the rise of populism, entrepreneurial energy will be invested in keeping this momentum going, exponentially. The summary findings suggest that research is scarce in an entrepreneurial setting, as extant research is based on large firms.

Since March (1991), the exploration and exploitation, and the balance thereof, developed an understanding that for a success of a firm, apart from other issues, a balancing act between the exploration of new possibilities and the exploitation of old certainties drives the twin pillars of new products and features on one hand, and profit maximization on the other. It has propelled managers' and CEOs' understanding that focussing only on exploitation results in a sure way to failure in the long run, as evidenced by Nokia's mobile phone business failure. On the other hand, many innovative approaches fall short of cashflow generation, because they are in the exploration trap. Neither the first approach of too much exploitation, nor the later process of too much exploration, is right. Many authors listed in Table 1 proposed the same message, but only until 2009, when a new approach in understanding the need for a balancing act of operation, as relative exploration became a reality in a longitudinal setting in large firms. There is an optimum range, in an inverted U-shaped relationship, between relative exploration and long-term firm performance (Uotila et al. 2009), suggesting that the sweet spot lies in the middle-range values of relative exploration (operationalized as exploration divided by the total of exploration and exploitation activities or efforts). These benefits with robust technology focus with R&D would be highly beneficial as well. Thus, the top management and middle management's strategic orientations and attention must create a culture that can harness these dichotomies' benefits where technological change drives the future.

Though these studies were done in large firm or SME settings, the process of balancing these complicated dichotomies could also be used in small firm settings, but merged with startup discourse, as suggested by lean start-up. Nevertheless, to bring the readers abreast of the current reality also encouraged me to build Tables 1, 2, and 3 as a summary of existing literature to develop the theoretical model in Chapter 3. Though Chapter 3 anchors the model from my earlier book chapter, we cannot deny that literature has a wide gap in fulfilling the understanding of entrepreneurial exploration and exploitation, and the balancing act thereof.

The emergence of i4.0 makes entrepreneurs vulnerable on the one hand, but makes them empowered on the other. Thus, this book's essence rests in harnessing this change's benefits while understanding and minimizing the harm or vulnerabilities created by the technological shift. As with any change, this will also unfreeze society and shake the current paradigms and dogmas first. There will be a resistance to change, and the valley of despair and death will last for a long time. However, all layoffs and unrest will go away when the positive benefits outweigh the negative impacts.

**Table 1. Literature Review of Entrepreneurial Exploration and Exploitation to Derive Implications for i4.0** (Adapted from Bhandari, 2017)

| **Author(s)** | **Findings** |
|---|---|
| March (1991) | Exploration is good for the short run but self-destructive in the long run. Balancing both creates a competitive advantage. Turnover is good for knowledge creation, and the slow socialization of new employees helps create variability in knowledge creation. |
| Ireland, Hitt, and Sirmon (2003) | Authors think that SE balances both opportunities seeking and advantage seeking approaches. |
| Gibson and Birkinshaw (2004) | Supported the mediating role of Relative Exploration |

| | |
|---|---|
| Gupta, Smith, and Shalley (2006) | Future research agenda: first, micro-level studies are very scarce; second, multiple levels of analysis are not many; third, the challenges associated with the balancing of both (ambidexterity vs. punctuated equilibrium) |
| Lavie and Rosenkopf (2006) | Absorptive capacity and organizational inertia have an impact on exploration and exploitation. Despite the path dependencies, firms balance their tendencies to explore and exploit over time and across domains. |
| Venkatraman, Lee and Iyer (2007) | Authors find that sequential ambidexterity significantly predicts sales growth as the main effect, as well as jointly with a set of contingency effects. |
| Bierly and Daly (2007) | A linear relationship exists between exploration and value creation. A concave relationship exists between exploitation and value creation. This has a managerial implication that, after a point, focusing on exploitation leads to reduced returns. A competitive environment's moderating effect is stronger in stable and high-tech environments than in dynamic and low-tech environments. The relationship between exploration and value creation is higher in high-tech environments compared to low-tech environments. |
| Raisch and Birkinshaw (2008) | Organizational antecedents: structure, context, leadership. OA: Organizational learning, innovation, organizational adaptation, strategic management, corporate design. Moderators: environmental dynamism, competitive dynamics, MO, resource endowment, and firm scope. Outcome: Accounting, market, and growth. |
| O'Reilly and Tushman (2008) | The senior team's substantive roles are most important. |
| Quintana-García and Benavides-Velasco (2008) | Exploratory innovative capability is more critical for technological diversification than exploitative capability. |
| Raisch, Birkinshaw, Probst, and Tushman (2009) | Longitudinal research is suggested. Need for dynamic perspectives. Multiple levels of analysis are presented. Moderating conditions for positive value creation such as size and resource endowment, environmental dynamism, and industry contexts. |
| Lavie, Stettner, and Tushman (2010) | Balance via organizational or temporal separation; balance via domain separation; contingency approach for balancing effects. Use of single continuous variable to capture exploration-exploitation. Balance with a quadratic function that reaches a maximum value at an intermediate point. Compare and contrast multiple operationalizations. |

| | |
|---|---|
| Hitt, Ireland, Sirmon and Trahms (2011) | Multilevel outcomes. |
| Sirén, Kohtamäki and Kuckertz (2012) | Supported the hypotheses. |
| Junni, Sarala, Taras and Tarba (2013) | OA is essential for non-manufacturing industries, primarily when perceptual value creation measure is used and in a cross-sectional design. |
| O'Reilly and Tushman (2013) | Findings resonate with Chen and Katila (2008), "Exploration and exploitation need not always be competing activities but can and should be complementary" (p208). Definitional issues should be addressed, ambidexterity should be conceptualized as a dynamic capability. "In this way, relative exploration (sequential, simultaneous, or contextual) is reflected in a complex set of decisions and routines that enable the organization to sense and seize new opportunities through the reallocation of organizational assets" (p17). Future research should look into distributed innovation and balancing of exploration and exploitation. |
| Birkinshaw and Gupta (2013) | Brought the perspective to the field of ambidexterity, requesting a greater focus. Critical areas for unique contributions are: a) where to juxtaposition the efficiency frontier? B) How to reach the efficiency frontier? c) how to push the efficiency frontier out? |
| Lisboa, Skarmeas and Lages (2013) | The effect of exploration is positive, while the impact of exploration is negative. Focus on the high turbulence and shows balancing of exploration and exploitation effects. |
| Stettner and Lavie (2014) | Balancing across modes a firm can avoid detriments to value creation. Balance across modes is essential compared to balance within modes. Key finding: exploring via externally oriented modes such as acquisition or alliances, while exploiting via internal organization enhances the firm value creation. |

The direct relationship between balancing exploration and exploitation outlined in Table 1 has been augmented by mediation and moderation models, as shown in Table 2. This suggests that aligning the business with environmental reality is a must, and contingency theory must be the theoretical lens in understanding this phenomenon. Other similar variables may moderate the relationship between balancing exploration and exploitation and firm performance from corporate governance to technology strategy and centralization and formalization.

**Table 2. Ambidexterity literature on interaction effects (Adapted from Bhandari 2017)**

| Author(s) | Findings |
| --- | --- |
| Lubatkin, Simsek, Ling and Veiga (2006) | CEO is pivotal in achieving ambidexterity. |
| Rothaermel and Alexandre (2009) | Technology sourcing mix<-value creation is an inverted U-shape. ACAP moderates positively. |
| Simsek, Heavey, Veiga, and Souder (2009) | A two-by-two typology delineates four types described as harmonic, cyclical, partitioned, and reciprocal ambidexterity based on temporal and structural dimensions. Need for mediation and moderation studies. |
| Jansen, van den Bosch and Volberda (2006) | Centralization <- exploratory innovation (DV) (-ve). Formalization <- exploitative innovation (DV) (+ve). Connectedness is an important antecedent to both types of innovations. Exploratory innovation<-for dynamic environments. Exploitative innovation <- for a competitive environment. |

Though there is some understanding of antecedents and moderators' performance impact, there is still confusion on measuring exploration, exploitation, and the balance thereof, as shown in Table 3. Some of the authors have used the balance of exploration and exploitation as a product of exploration and exploitation measures. Some have used it as the balance of the two, and others have used it as the addition of the two. Thus, the measurement approaches of exploration, exploitation, and balance have differing shapes and results when modeled through the relationship with the firm performance. This anomaly sometimes makes the readers' understanding of the phenomenon confusing. As the research process goes further, at some point, common-sense among authors may emerge in theory, measurement, and analysis methods, so that a common approach to tackling this dilemma will become easier. When we discuss the balance of exploration and exploitation, we will use relative exploration (Uotila et al. 2009) as a measurement approach.

**Table 3. Measures of Balancing Exploration and Exploitation (Adapted from Bhandari, 2017)**

| *OA Measured as a product.* | *OA Measured as balance.* | *OA Measured as an addition.* |
|---|---|---|
| Gibson and Birkinshaw (2004) | He and Wong (2004) | Lubatkin, Simsek, Ling and Veiga (2006) |
| Tiwana (2008) | Lin, Yang and Demirkan (2007) | Jansen, Tempelaar, van den Bosch and Volberda (2009) |
| Im and Rai (2008) | Rothaermel and Alexandre (2009) | Cao, Simsek, and Zhang (2010) |
| Jansen, George, Van Den Bosch and Volberda (2008) | Fernhaber and Patel (2012) | |
| Morgan and Berthon (2008) | Boumgarden, Nickerson and Zenger (2012) | |
| Cao, Gedajlovic and Zhang (2009) | | |
| Jansen, Simsek and Cao (2012) | | |
| Tushman, Smith, Wood, Westerman, and O'Reilly (2010) | | |
| Hill and Birkinshaw (2012) | | |

## SOLUTIONS AND RECOMMENDATIONS

Porter's (1985) argument is that technological innovations may have impacts on a firm's strategic choices, which in turn may change the industry at large as well. However, one cannot generalize that technological change is always useful. The wisdom lies not only in adopting technological change, but also in understanding the timing of its implementation. As the new wave of multiple technologies evolves, not all changes will be beneficial. The firms have the absorptive capacity to adapt to the new dynamics of new or emerging business models, smart, interconnected products, real-time optimization, and balancing both exploration and exploitation.

Porter and Heppelmann (2014) suggest that information technology is changing the current reality of product development. The old paradigm, based on mechanical and electrical parts in a product, is challenged, as new complex systems which combine software and hardware, sensors, data storage, microprocessors, and connectivity, in multiple ways, have become a reality. The emergence of these 'smart, connected products' will use the available good processing power, and device miniaturization enabled by modularity in the design and network benefits, of ubiquitous wireless connectivity. These changes will be so large that the locus of innovation, competition, and entrepreneurial attention, will have huge implications.

While Porter and Heppelmann (2014) touched on the implications outside the firm's boundary, Porter and Heppelmann (2015) do so for inside the firm's periphery. The change brought about by i4.0 does not only change the competition dynamics, industry rivalry, and for that matter, innovation and entrepreneurship; it also changes the business we are in today. The past products and business models will not be sufficient to survive in this new world order. Thus, the way the transformed, smart, connected products influence every manufacturing firm's function is crucial. While manufacturing goes through its transformations, so does the entrepreneurial ecosystem, to support this change.

Perhaps inhouse innovation will not be able to solve or adapt to the new reality. Existing manufacturers must embrace the latest solutions pushed by a new generation of visionary and tech-savvy entrepreneurs. The value chain which gave us modern thinking in management education is under transformation from product development, IT, manufacturing, logistics, marketing, sales, and after-sales service. This transformation makes a new definition of these roles as the coordination and collaboration intensity amongst these internal functions determines the newly transformed firm's successor; the newly established venture. Perhaps data science-types of functions will emerge in the new age, which will have significant implications for the structure and decision making at the same time. This change will be the first-ever since the second industrial revolution. Let us ride the wave with an open mind and alertness to evolve as the i4.0 era evolves. However, being a step ahead of this change will take us further, more easily.

While the role of technology has changed, Michael Porter's strategy (Porter 1980) and competitiveness-related concepts are still relevant (Stonehouse and Snowdon 2007). His lasting contributions to strategy have been tested against time, academic rigor, and accessibility to managers. However, as Porter and Heppelman (2014, 2015) attempted to revisit his seminal concepts on strategy and competitiveness, the emerging implications for management, strategy, and changing industry boundaries suggest that researchers need to explore these new dynamics with an open mind to assess the emerging challenges and manage the technological change for the benefit of humankind. While many research domains may emerge, my quest is to understand the entrepreneurial exploration and exploitation trade-off in i4.0. In doing so, I asked a few relevant questions on why existing entrepreneurship models fall short, and why the new wave needs to develop a new approach to understand innovation, management, and strategy in a larger context.

As illustrated above, extant literature suggests that existing entrepreneurship models fall short in understanding the emerging nature of i4.0 related changes. We need models that adapt to the changing process itself, and preplanned approaches do not hold in the dynamic industry. As discussed in Chapter 1, Sarasvathy's (2001) approach to opportunity creation might be a fruitful decision-making tool that has been side-lined from the *Harvard Business Review* models on lean start-up. The emergent nature of means orientation, though with a vision, brings feedback loops in learning and adaptation, as and when the change unfolds.

Another issue raised in Chapter 1 argues, for example, an outline of Burmeister, Lüttgens, and Piller's (2016) emerging new business models supported by i4.0 and platform-based business models. Creating a business model is easy, but implementation and support for the same is a daunting task. It is a new paradigm, and it is changing everything we know as in business so far. We need new best practices to surf this sea of change, build new organizational structures to align the difference with the new reality, build necessary tools to analyse, optimize, and understand the technology layer, plus its impact on the firm's business model.

Collaboration, competition, and communication across firm boundaries will be the need of the hour for stakeholders. Having resource-based advantages created by valuable, rare, inimitable, and non-substitutable (VRIN) resources (Barney 1991) may have its place in cross-border alliances and collaboration and platform economy as suggested by Lavie (2006). The time is ripe for upheaval in transforming manufacturing industries into a bundle of services with premium, differentiated products and services with customized solutions to customers' demands. The research frontier calling for researchers is still in infancy. A new innovative business model, efficiency projects, and implications for theory and research of management are on the verge of emergence.

We need to understand the relationships between business model alternatives, competitive strategy, and the resulting performance outcomes in the new industrial internet wave. The changes suggested by Burmeister et al. (2016) have some exciting implications for management theory and practice. The new wave offers the possibility for customization of products and services and efficiency optimization at the same time. This will give an edge for those who understand the meaning of adaptation to individual customer needs.

Porter's idea of competitive supremacy based on only either cost leadership or differentiation is being challenged. The new change wave will delete the concept of stuck-in-the-middle syndrome while pursuing both cost leadership and differentiation. The old idea of 'red ocean'-based cut-throat competition is no more valid, while the new 'blue ocean' thinking where competition is irrelevant is becoming a reality. As business level thinking is changing, so does functional level thinking; balancing the trade-off between novelty-centricity and efficiency-centricity (Zott and Amit 2007) in business model design is becoming a reality, as illustrated by multiple cases by Burmeister et al. (2016). Thus, both entrepreneurial exploration and exploitation are possible at the same time.

While I am teaching, I use straightforward existing communication channels like Facebook Messenger to communicate with students (customers). This almost-real-time communication has enhanced learning skills and customer satisfaction levels and helped build brand ambassadors for the university. Imagine the future classroom, online learning materials, and connected universities in real-time to deliver a new experience to the classroom and learning solutions. Suppose this is happening in the service sector. In that case, sensor-enabled products' power will revolutionize the customer experience — even though we need to fix privacy and security issues at its core. Changes in distribution channels and customer relations empowered by bots and AI will be a new frontier in understanding the customer better and saving costs simultaneously. The concept of B2B is changing into B2B2C as manufacturers are getting live data from the smart products directly, and the new platform business is already knocking on the doors of customers. For companies, embracing the open business model suggested by Chesbrough (2006) might be a good strategy as networks and platforms with blurred boundaries will be a new reality.

**Business Model Innovation Process**. In the past, my own experience in the multinational and start-up world infers that the business model innovation (BMI) process generally resides with the product development department or team. The changing reality of i4.0-triggered innovation is not restricted only to the single product level or department. This demands the BMI process must be run at the CEO, or top management team, level. It crosses all boundaries (inside or outside) and needs partnerships and alliances, moving away from competitive supremacy to competitive supremacy where all stakeholders are respected. Customer shared value (CSV) (Porter and Kramer 2019) is possible. The founder's attention across the functions and the firm boundaries with multiple stakeholders since inception is needed for start-ups. Without this platform thinking, harnessing the benefits of i4.0 technologies will fall short.

However, policymakers must be vigilant that no one becomes a monopoly or duopoly in any circumstances, and the formation of a cartel must be avoided. The idea behind the separation of business model innovation and product development is based on the logic that traditional product development processes follow stage-gate processes. BMI in the new era needs to follow agile, lean start-up, customer development, iteration, scrum design thinking, and hypothesis-based development. Detailed discussions on this new frontier will be covered in the customer creation chapter ("The competitive advantage of interconnected firms: An extension of the resource-based view" (Lavie, D., *Academy of Management Review* 2006, Vol. 31(3), 638-658).

Though the resource-based view (RBV) Barney (1991) created a firm foundation for the VRIN resources as the basis of sustainable competitive advantage, Lavie (2006) extended the RBV for interconnected firms where network resources determine the competitive supremacy of the interconnected firms or platforms. Leveraging of value across the boundaries of the firm is distinguished by the shared resources from nonshared resources. Also, there are multiple options in generating rent. In terms of the role of firm-, relation-, and partner-specific factors in making network resources into contributing factors to capture value from such an alliance network, RBV becomes an extended-RBV where the assessment shows that heterogeneity, imperfect mobility, imitability, and substitutability of a resource is valuable and rare. In this assessment, relational resources matter more than the nature of resources in the alliance or platform network.

The value and rareness of physical, intellectual, informational, or financial resources will no longer be the success mantra in the era of i4.0. It is all about building a trust-based relationship in the participating network. Due to social media's virality, any mistakes in online information privacy and security would trigger the failure curve's downward spiral. Therefore, nurturing the relational aspect, and building this as a dynamic capability to sense, seize, and orchestrate such an interconnected network, is necessary. Thus, relational capability and network resources become the next goldmine in the platform business. Whether we like it or not, even a process automation firm is vulnerable to such a transformation, never mind the product or service business firm.

An exciting aspect of Lavie (2006) is that the rents from the perspective of the focal firms could be considered in a balanced way, as there are inbound and outbound effects in the rent-generating capacity of the alliance or platform business in a discussion (refer to figure in Lavie, 2006). When the focal firm uses its share and nonshared resources, it is called internal rent extraction. However, when both partners' shared resources are used, then, in this condition, only the relational rent could be extracted. On the other hand, if a partner's shared and nonshared resources generate rent, it is called inbound spillover rent, whereas if the focal firm uses its resources, it is called outbound spillover rent.

However, while using AI, Vuori et al. (forthcoming) suggest that, ironically, artificial intelligence tools may increase your biases in strategic decision-making if proper understanding and use is not comprehended. While generating rent through such an optimization algorithm, there is a risk that we just become like a competitor we are monitoring, or, if we have a supervised learning approach in AI and machine learning, we only improve on what we have. Still, if we go for multiple options, the options simulation will cause paralysis by analysis. In such an approach, radical disruption and business models may be sidelined. Therefore, a caution of note in understanding the risk of being blinded by the obvious may be essential early enough. In this book, an attempt has been made by introducing an unfair advantage into i4.0BMC to keep room for radical breakthrough and sustainable competitive advantage created by network resources and competitive supremacy in contrast to competitive supremacy.

As pioneered by Android, it is interesting to see how exploiting and defending open digital platforms with boundary resources is possible through Android's five platform forks (Karhu, Gustafsson, and Lyytinen, 2018). This enables innovation and value generation, as evidenced by Lavie (2006). Such platforms' boundary resources could be an API, and AppStore allows complements for the platform to be developed and shared. Another approach could be to use an open-source license as a boundary resource to open and share the platform's core resources. As shown in Figure 1, entrepreneurial exploration, exploitation, and platform rent as an ecosystem of concepts and theories suggest that we need to evolve above Barney's VRIN resources. Karhu et al. (2018) note that over-comprehensive openness may lead to vulnerability of strategic exploitation. This is called platform forking, and, in this process, a competing platform could be created by the exploiters. Google has managed such forking and has modified Android's boundary resources to curb exploitation and retain control. Karhu et al. (2018) argue that the theory of competitive advantage of the open digital platform could be the cornerstones of protection from such platform forking. Building a cooperative governance mechanism to combat such platform forking would enable sustained competitive advantage of the platform. Though Amazon built its Fire platform by doing platform forking over the Android, Android later built its defense mechanism through relational rent rather than VRIN resources as suggested by Barney (1991). Karhu et al. (2018) argue following Dyer and Singh (1998) to understand the relational view of competitive advantage, similar, but in contrast to Lavie (2006).

According to Barney (1991) and information systems capabilities (Bharadwaj 2000), as discussed earlier, building a cooperative governance mechanism may curtail such behaviour, and collectively the alliance partners defend platform forking. The cooperative perspective of platform strategy becomes a guiding principle in line with the complementarities and network effects (Koch and Windsperger 2017), where boundary resources such as an app store and an API guide the complementors and platform owners to extract appropriated relational rents, as suggested by Lavie (2006). In this process, an internal rent is generated through the user data. Google uses proprietary machine-learning algorithms to extract this internal rent based on the user data and its advertising business preferences. To conclude:

> "Apple has maximized internal rents from its proprietary resources. Avoiding openness, except while tapping into critical appropriated relational rents from app complements, has protected itself against outbound spill over rents. Google, by contrast, following a more open platform strategy, has sought to maximize appropriated relational rents but at the same time has exposed itself to the threat of outbound spill over rents realized through platform forks" (Karhu et al. 2018, 492).

**Implications for entrepreneurial exploration.** At the heart of this change is the possibility for the simultaneous pursuit of opportunity discovery and creation, which has divided academicians for over a decade. While building open innovation models with customers and partners, the exploration crosses the firm and industry boundaries. Who knew a social network like Facebook could get into the money business through its Libra? Similarly, the value creation is happening at a high rate, supported by competence in i4.0 technologies across the firm, from the top to the factory floor.

**Implications for entrepreneurial exploitation.** Over the years, the nurturing of ICT has benefitted efficiency projects; however, it will be different this time. While leveraging optimization algorithms in manufacturing and resource allocation, vast benefits come from the new ideas and processes that may become the cornerstone of competitive advantage or, for that matter, sustainable advantages where all stakeholders benefit from each other. To succeed, a new culture of experimentation, celebrating failure as part of learning, and a meritocracy based on i4.0 skills, must be the focus of the culture, as 'culture eats strategy for breakfast'.

**Implications for balancing exploration and exploitation and performance.** The publication of a seminal paper by March (1991) to help understand the organizational learning from the lens of balancing exploration and exploitation was the starting point in this stream of literature. Since then, the very concept of balancing exploration and exploitation has been studied in multiple ways with various sets of definitions, new conceptualizations, measurements, and numerous forms of applying the concept to get its living course (Almahendra and Ambos 2015).

I am repeating the core definitional issues here once again. The organizational issues and activities classified as exploration are search, variation, risk-taking, experimentation, play, flexibility, discovery, and innovation (March

1991, 71). Similarly, exploitation includes issues and activities as refinement, choice, production, efficiency, selection, implementation, and execution (March 1991, 71). When issues and activities are search-oriented, and managers are allowed to take a risk, conduct an experiment, invest in flexibility, discovery, and then innovation, an organization positions itself as an innovative company. In such an environment, 'culture eats strategy for breakfast'. People are self-driven with a clear focus to come up with a new business model, unfair advantages, platformization, and open innovation.

Similarly, when an organization's issues and activities are cognizant of refining a product or process, building multiple options in products and services, driven by an efficiency mantra with a relentless focus on execution as a capability, then the organization positions itself as an efficiency-driven firm. People are driven by short-term profit in such ventures. However, the beauty lies in the founder's delicate balancing act of both types of activities.

Large firms' research in balancing these exploration and exploitation-related activities and their dynamics have been significantly understood. However, research in balancing the two delicate dilemmas in entrepreneurial ventures is scarce, to my knowledge. This is fundamentally the reason for significant start-up failures. They are in a 'failure-trap', as they are busy with exploration, and they are not good at exploitation at the right time. Or they are scaling up prematurely when they need to pivot. Even the strategic choices for entrepreneurial exploration and exploitation are challenging to solve, as the runway for the start-up survival is usually too small compared to the large firm context, and the competition for a scarce resource is very high. There is no room for too much - or too little – exploitation; rowing this boat with both hands is necessary to sail it to safe harbor amidst the ever-changing reality where change is the only constant.

## CONCLUSION

The search for a new dependent variable will outline the full further research agenda in a later chapter, but to understand how institutions make entrepreneurial exploration and exploitation better or worse is important. Though we have touched upon building innovative and quality culture, it would take a separate book to untangle the idea that 'culture eats strategy for breakfast'. This book only focuses on exploration and exploitation as antecedents at this stage. As culture could be a separate book, so could the moderation and mediation models while linking exploration and exploitation to performance. Extant literature used accounting-based metrics to measure performance, while this book introduced CLV as a dependent variable. Therefore, further research in entrepreneurial settings with this new variable as a dependent would be vital in untangling the dichotomies of exploration and exploitation in an entrepreneurial environment.

A new wave of applications based on unique technologies embedded into i4.0 would be an exciting avenue for further research. For example, 5G network slicing might be a useful research agenda in linking multiple factories and smoothing interconnectivity and processing features which may increase network usage and optimization algorithms. Similarly, the IoT, and cloud-based optimization could open a new frontier of research in untangling the understanding of how both cost and differentiation could be realized in each platform business, and the Porterian view of strategic purity as the only strategic posture becomes the thing of the past.

Rajan (2015) admits that arguing against capitalism is a bit like a fish analysing water. However, unless, and until, a new wave entrepreneur who can balance both exploration and exploitation continue to focus on the 'triple P' benefits of profit, planet, and people, current civilization threatens to dry up the entire pond. However, existing notions of lean start-up, the Customer Development Model, and the Business Model, must be adapted to meet the demands of changes enabled by i4.0. As a preparation, in Chapters 1 and 2, we have outlined a thesis on why this imperative is needed and introduced the basic blocks (except for the Business Model Canvas). The following chapter fills this gap and discusses all three models and modifications: lean start-up, the Customer Development Model, and the Business Model Canvas.

In doing so, we are equally conscious of social and eco-entrepreneurs as the future of capitalism's proponents. Let us build a sustainable future and meet United Nations' Sustainable Development Goals (SDGs). However, in calling for entrepreneurs to pursue this lofty goal, the whole book is designed to optimize CLV rather than SDGs. Still, if an entrepreneur measures progress with CLV, the realization of SDGs would be more comfortable, as current customers are increasingly aware of brands that respect society and climate at the same time. Let us plan for another book on the SDGs as an optimization approach, but for now, accept the limitations of the outcome variable being the CLV.

## REFERENCES

Almahendra, R., and Ambos, B. (2015). Exploration and exploitation: a 20-year review of evolution and reconceptualization. *International Journal of Innovation Management*, *19*(01), 1550008.

Blank, S. (2005). *The four steps to Epiphany*, CafePress.

Burmeister, C., Lüttgens, D., and Piller, F. T. (2016). Business model innovation for Industrie 4.0: why the "Industrial Internet" mandates a new perspective on innovation. *Die Unternehmung*, *70*(2), 124-152.

Karhu, K., Gustafsson, R., and Lyytinen, K. (2018). Exploiting and defending open digital platforms with boundary resources: Android's five platform forks. *Information Systems Research*, *29*(2), 479-497.

Lavie, D. (2006). The competitive advantage of interconnected firms: An extension of the resource-based view. *Academy of management review*, *31*(3), 638-658.

Lavie, D., and Rosenkopf, L. (2006). Balancing exploration and exploitation in alliance formation. *Academy of Management Journal*, *49*(4), 797-818.

Mason, P. (2016). *Postcapitalism: A guide to our future*. Macmillan.

Phelps, E. S. (2013). *Mass flourishing: How grassroots innovation created jobs, challenge, and change*. Princeton University Press.

Porter, M. E. (1985). Technology and competitive advantage. *Journal of Business Strategy*, *5*(3), 60-78.

Porter, M. E., and Kramer, M. R. (2019). Creating shared value. In *managing a sustainable business* (pp. 323-346). Springer, Dordrecht.

Rajan, S. (2015). *A tale of two capitalisms: sacred economics in nineteenth-century Britain*. University of Michigan Press.

Rajan, R. G., and Zingales, L. (2004). Saving capitalism from the capitalists: Unleashing the power of financial markets to create wealth and spread opportunity. Princeton University Press.

Stonehouse, G., and Snowdon, B. (2007). Competitive advantage revisited: Michael Porter on strategy and competitiveness. *Journal of Management Inquiry*, *16*(3), 256-273.

## KEY TERMS AND DEFINITIONS

**Entrepreneurial exploration:** The process of innovation, search, explore and build new products or services.

**Entrepreneurial exploitation:** The process of efficiency, automation, and optimization of existing products or services or the early phase of new products or services.

**Industry 4.0 (i4.0):** A new industrial wave generated due to the collective technologies such as 5G, cloud computing, machine learning, artificial intelligence, and internet of things (IoT), etc

**Ethnocentric:** A belief that one's own culture is superior to other cultures. The abbreviation frequently used is i4.0.

**I4.0BMC:** Business model canvas adapted to industry 4.0 changes.

# CHAPTER 3

# INDUSTRY 4.0 BUSINESS MODEL: SEARCH AND EXECUTION


## ABSTRACT

*Entrepreneurial exploration and exploitation and balancing the two to search for a new business model and execute the business model extant literature uses a customer development model, or lean start-up. Departing from earlier literature, we embedded lean start-up concepts into the broader framework of jobs-to-be-done theory (Christensen et al. 2016). Due to the industry 4.0 wave, the change we are envisaging in each industry's business model demands some modifications in the build-measure-learn (BML) loop, which needs to be augmented by the build-measure-optimize-learn (BMOL) loop. This chapter is taking optimization as algorithm-based, and AI and machine learning-enabled, which gives real-time adjustments of field parameters so that the possibility to explore and exploit simultaneously is a reality. The entire discourse under the business model canvas shows that the customer development model changes, though we have kept those model's boxes and skeleton almost identical to minor modifications. As discussed in Chapter 2, the book will be based on creating relational rent in open innovation and platformization, as enabled by i4.0. This change has a massive implication for policymakers and practitioners alike, and academicians may have a perpetual research agenda as i4.0 evolves further.*



Keywords: Industry 4.0, Business model search, Business model execution, BMOL

## INTRODUCTION

The starting point of this chapter is to define i4.0. Various technical definitions or components are available to understand this umbrella concept, such as value chain, smart factory, competitiveness, strategy, and the Internet of Things. However, the principal change agent in all of these components is the Internet of Things. The IoT is defined as:

> "…a conceptual framework that leverages on the availability of heterogeneous devices and interconnection solutions, as well as augmented physical objects providing a shared information base on a global scale, to support the design of applications involving at the same virtual level both people and representations of objects" (Atzori et al. 2010, 137).

However, being comprehensive in IoT is not a synonym of i4.0. It crosses the IoT and touches AI, cloud computing, 5G, blockchain, and other emerging technologies. The emergence of i4.0 technologies, together with 5G, heralds a new era in human progress and civilization. The implication of the change seems so big, some of the proponents of AI have even claimed that 'AI is the next electricity'. If AI is equivalent to electricity in the disruptions and progress it is embodying, we are on the cusp of getting to a singularity where machines will be more intelligent than humans, sooner rather than later. However, a human can unplug the entire AI or i4.0 network in a case of an attack of the machines. With this perspective, it is a significant undertaking to participate in this progress trajectory. This book delves into entrepreneurial exploration and exploitation as a theoretical lens to dissect the practitioner's contributions such as lean start-up, Customer Development Model, or Business Model Canvas (BMC). In attempting to do so, we are not claiming to rewrite the claims the earlier literature has made. On the other hand, the attempt is to rethink all the flesh around the skeleton we have in the models mentioned above.

In this emerging situation, the build-measure-learn BML loop of lean start-up is modified with the build-measure-optimize-learn (BMOL) loop. The Business Model Canvas (BMC) has a new version called i4.0 Business Model Canvas (i4.0BMC). However, the process of discovering customer, customer validation, and pivot or persevere decisions, is intact in philosophical terms. The same applies to customer creation and company building suggested by Blank (2013). While revisiting these concepts from the theoretical lens of entrepreneurial exploration and exploitation may seem trivial at first, combining the lens with the changes happening in i4.0 technologies makes the book interesting. Before embarking upon this book project, being an engineer myself, I had never thought through the implications of the i4.0 wave. This wave's unprecedented change and potential for prosperity demand attention from the best of the best minds.

Apart from other concepts that the chapter will elaborate on below, the notion of i4.0BMC and the embedded nature of unfair advantages as the main driving force in creating a new business model for start-ups makes the focus clear and concrete. The solutions that emerge using i4.0 technologies in solving the mega problems of the world will have massive potential in transforming industry after industry. Blurring industry boundaries and functional silos in internal organizations will be so powerful in planning, organizing, staffing/leading, and controlling, that the future of management will never be the same. Let us embrace this reality with an open and alert mind to minimize the change's pitfalls and maximize the positive impact.

## BACKGROUND

The majority of the tools and models we discuss in this book mainly come from entrepreneurial practice. However, observing these tools and models from a proven theoretical lens, such as balancing exploration and exploitation becomes interesting from the academic perspective. The practitioners have a rigorous analysis of their models. They can learn from the missing links inside the models. The i4.0 technologies are many, thus comprehending their nature in a single book is a daunting task. However, we use the changes triggered by such technologies as a guide, rather than understanding the architecture and each business model triggered by such change. To cater to that need, we will first delve into the Customer Development Model and modify it to suit our purpose. Apart from introducing decision logic suggested by Sarasvathy (2001) on effectuation and causation, it also brings Bricolage into the discussion under the decision-making chapter, which was implicit or non-existing in earlier decision models. We then redraw the BMOL loop to replace the BML loop in lean start-up thinking, where the 'O' means optimization based on real-time data and data science behind the cloud. The guiding tool for all these models is BMC, and we are going to draw i4.0BMC and use it as a guideline throughout the book.

Existing entrepreneurial search models used in practice by entrepreneurs have not yet been empirically tested in rigorous academic research. However, similar approaches with different conceptions and beliefs have been around in academic literature. Two of these concepts, which resemble the business model's search and execution suggested by the customer development model, are entrepreneurial exploration and exploitation, and effectuation and causations. The later approaches have filled enough academic journal pages to build confidence, but the same evidence with these original names has been missing in the start-up world. Perhaps no one has yet bridged the gap between journal publications and consulting based on these rigorous studies.

In this book, the mapping of existing general practices with that of academic research is attempted. In doing so, as a core academician but with a background in start-ups and multinationals, I may be best suited to build the links. However, I am aware of the challenges and criticisms that may follow after the publication of this book. I trust that academicians and entrepreneurs alike will find this bridging attempt worth the effort. They may benefit by creating their own unfair advantages anchored in the updated models suggested by the book.

## ENTREPRENEURIAL EXPLORATION AND EXPLOITATION IN SEARCH AND EXECUTION OF THE BUSINESS MODEL

### Issues, Controversies, Problems

When March (1991) introduced the concept of exploration and exploitation, he simply said that when we conduct activities such as search, experiment, and innovate, we are exploring, while when we carry out activities such as being efficient, optimization, and automation, we are exploiting. The idea here is so powerful that many companies fail due to the exploitation trap, as they are driven by short-term profit and share price, and they forget to invest in innovation and exploration. While this is the reality of large firms, start-ups do premature scaling driven by the exploitation trap, as they need to generate cash in a rapid time. Otherwise, they will have no investment left to run the start-up further.

If this is the case for large corporations, the same problem lies in the startup world. We have seen stories on both the exploration and exploitation traps in the entrepreneurial world. Usually, in the old paradigm, establishing a new venture is solely based on entrepreneurial vision and the execution of that vision using millions of dollars of investment, which does not survive the first customer contact. In this case, we have not experimented with customers early enough. Even if we did, we did it on the conceptual level through market research. What is needed is the early test of minimum viable products, and the belief that both exploration and exploitation can go side by side. Suppose this is the reality in the business model search phase. In that case, the same thing happens in the business model execution phase, where premature scaling or hunger for early exploitation leads the start-up astray. The failure rate in Silicon Valley is 9 out of 10 in the old entrepreneurial paradigm, and the new breeds of processes and tools are claiming it to reduce this to 7 out of 10 failings, which gives three successes for every 10 tries.

The following section discusses the model in detail that might result, as and when i4.0 technologies evolve in developing smart, interconnected products with real-time intelligence. This revolutionary business model search and execution process may develop later into different shapes, depending on the change variables or the outcome variables. The old vanity metrics of accounting measures do not resemble the business model's new search and execution. As we learn from the first few implementations of i4.0 enabled businesses, we will further develop the models. But for now, whatever wisdom we have, we will elaborate on that at greater length. Sarasvathy (2001) countered the assumptions of artifacts such as firms/organizations and markets, and many existing practices in the entrepreneurial world defy existing economics and management theories. According to her, the explanation for the creation of such artifacts requires a concept known as effectuation. While existing economic and management theories are based on the causation model, which rests on prediction thinking, the entrepreneurial approach rests on control logic. In other words, causation-related review takes a particular effect as given, and focuses on selecting between means, such as goal orientation to create that effect. On the contrary, the process takes a set of means as given, and builds on those means by selecting possible effects. Causation models might be right in stable environments, but effectuation models are suitable in uncertain environments, such as entrepreneurial ventures.

Though the primary model presented below will not include effectuation vs. causation logic, it assumes that these models are implicit in i4.0BMC. Later in the decision chapter, effectuation and causation models will be explicitly presented. The failure of existing start-ups falls typically into using the wrong logic of causation where the planning school uses goal orientation and prediction models. However, with the emergence of the tools we have discussed, and the alignment of this book's focus with reality and academic flavour, we are on the cusp of the next wave of entrepreneurial approach, which may be long lasting and more successful. However, we are talking about an unknown future under conditions of extreme uncertainty. In such uncertainty, claiming a success rate would be futile, based on the current understanding of the future. However, a significant improvement is expected in these models, as is start-up success. The entrepreneurial world needs to move from prediction thinking to control logic. Let us believe effectuation will become a model that every entrepreneur understands, and stakeholders will create an opportunity that has unfair advantages over their competitors.

Another pioneering concept in management is the Dynamic Capabilities framework, and recently it has been linked with the business model (Teece 2018). The basic assumption rests on the idea that business models, dynamic capabilities, and strategy, are connected. Good dynamic capabilities, not only in sensing, seizing, and orchestrating opportunities and resources, but also in big data analytics, give an unfair advantage to entrepreneurial ventures in the i4.0 era, by building a business model that is robust and sustainable in the long run, as the new wave of technologies shape the future of the organizational structure by removing silos and building cross-functional teams and departments enabled by data analytics. Communication, decision-making, and delegation, become easier without losing control. Entrepreneurial exploration and exploitation as a dynamic capability could also be a plausible theoretical route through which to sail through the sea of i4.0, where the emergence of a 'blue ocean' strategy is possible by making the competition irrelevant and breaking the value-cost trade-offs.

When balancing entrepreneurial exploration and exploitation is regressed against firm performance, a curvilinear relationship is shown (see Figure 1). Too little, or too much, of a balancing act between entrepreneurial exploration and exploitation is not suitable for performance. When it is in the lower level of effort, and the balance is not perfect, performance is lacking. Similarly, when too much effort in the balancing act is made, the slope becomes negative, suggesting that a high balancing act is detrimental for the firm. A range between 0.4 to 0.8 is a sweet spot that entrepreneurial managers need to focus on to build the balance, as shown in Figure 1. This curvilinear relationship has been reported to register an even higher performance level when R&D efforts are increased. As the new wave of i4.0 will enable such R&D, the curve will register an even higher peak, and a higher range for balancing entrepreneurial exploration and exploitation activities.

The assumption behind such an exaggerated curve is based on the platformization, open innovation, and relational rent, created through the boundary resources created by the focal firm in alliance or complementary relationships with the contributors in the ecosystem. This brings us to the notion that cooperative arrangement and governance of the boundary resources in such platforms are crucial, as evidenced in Chapter 2, where the arguments to avoid platform forking were put forward (Karhu et al. 2018). Theorizing on open digital platforms (ODPs) through the lens of strategists demands that rent extraction at the relational level is not only a science, but an art (Lavie 2006).

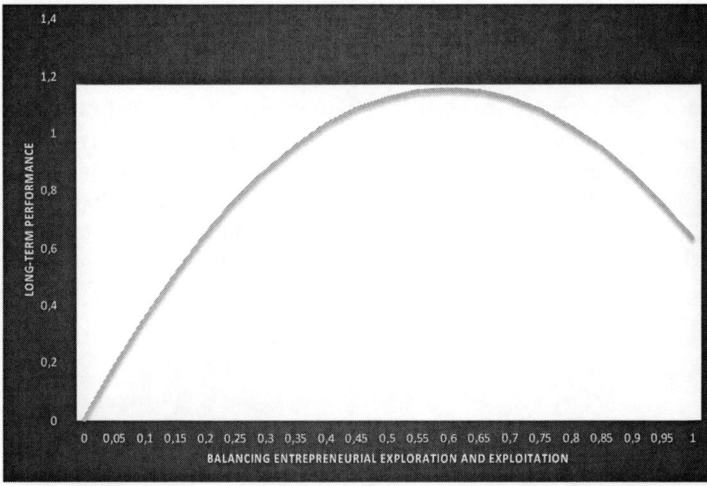


Figure 3-1. Performance impact of balancing entrepreneurial exploration and exploitation (adapted from Bhandari 2017)

## SOLUTIONS AND RECOMMENDATIONS

Bhandari (2018) proposed that the BML loop of Ries (2011) lean start-up should be modified to include 'optimize' as a distinct and explicit block, and argued that the age of i4.0 would be self-correcting. Both exploration and exploitation at the same time is possible if the entrepreneur wishes to harness it. When March (1991) proposed the idea of the exploitation trap and the failure of a corporation, he argued that usually, when a company executes a business model, the management is blinded by the obvious or short-termism driven by share price and quarterly results. This traditional accounting does not give importance to exploration, where the search for a business model is essential. While executing the Symbian-based business model, Nokia was left behind in the 3G business model, and they had to sell Nokia Mobile Phones altogether. To avoid such pitfalls, large corporations like GE have already embraced lean start-up with mixed results. The approach sees all firms as entrepreneurial ventures in the age of i4.0, and even having ‘entrepreneurial manager’ rather than ‘manager’ as a title in the larger firms. If this is the requirement, and if there is such optimization AI, machine learning, and cloud computing, having ‘Optimize’ as a crucial step in the BMOL loop is highly recommended, as shown in Figure 2.

As discussed in the context of the larger framework, the BMOL loop also gets its guiding theory to solve the jobs-to-be-done by the customers, or various use cases and storyboards related to scenario testing. In this core process, in earlier notions, more correlational attributes were collected. But now, with Christensen et al.’s (2016) approach, a causal link between the product or service and the customer’s buying behaviour is identified. This tool gives a strong foundation where the theory proposed in *Competing Against Luck* (Hall, Christensen, Dillon, and Duncan 2016) finally becomes feasible. According to the authors, it is more about understanding customers’ choice and their behaviour in making purchase decisions. This removes correlation in the process, and builds causality in the real sense.

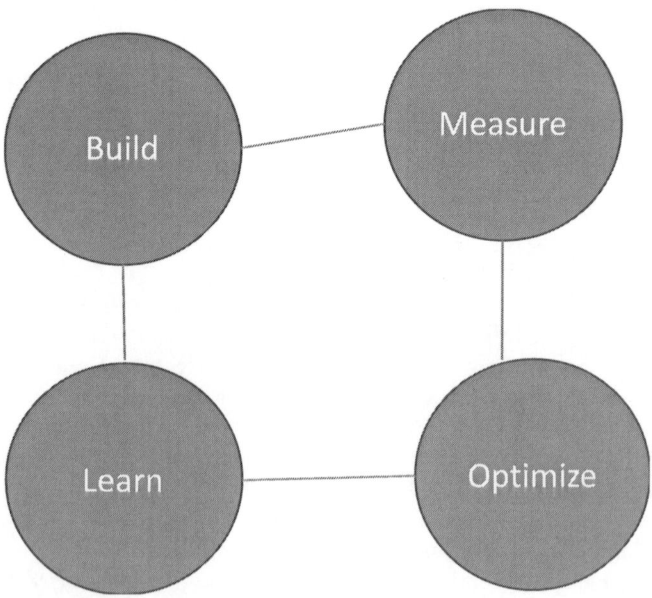


Figure 3-2. BMOL loop as a core element of entrepreneurial exploration and exploitation (author’s synthesis)

Using a guiding theory like jobs-to-be-done makes the next phase of the entrepreneurial wave far more exciting, while embedding it into the lean start-up concepts. However, with the theory's umbrella concept, the whole of lean testing and development gets a new meaning and hypotheses, building causality in the system from correlational attributes of customers' buying behavior.

While the cornerstone of entrepreneurial exploration and exploitation lies in my proposition of the BMOL loop, rather than the BML loop as suggested by extant literature, so the i4.0BMC plays a crucial role in the business model search and execution in the i4.0 world, rather than the old BMC suggested by Osterwalder (2010). In transitioning the processes to the next frontier, our assertion lies in the fact that CLV as a measure of success is mostly followed in this book for entrepreneurial exploration and exploitation-related benefits. While earlier literature is against accounting-based measures as a unit of progress, we have not abandoned that altogether. The focus on short-termism needs to shift away as i4.0BMC is optimized for for-profit and social-plus-environmental benefits, which are long-term goals of an organization.

First, to understand the customer discovery phase's primary value proposition, and test these hypotheses, including the growth hypothesis in the customer validation phase, i4.0 BMC becomes a guiding tool, as shown in Figure 3. With the umbrella of the exploration and exploitation dimension, BMOL loops are executed to search for a business model in early phases. Once the decision to build the full-scale product or service is reached, the business model execution phase starts, where customer creation and scaling up of the company become the new normal. While the search phase is predominantly exploration focussed, the execution phase is more exploitation oriented. However, as discussed in earlier sections, simultaneous exploration and exploitation are possible due to i4.0, and communication without delay, enabled by 5G, AI, cloud computing, IoT, and machine learning. As an example, two BMOL loops are shown in Figure 3, suggesting that the faster the loop, the better the startup in balancing entrepreneurial exploration and exploitation. This could also be real, based on the experiential learning of founders and teams in startups.

During the search phase, or even in the execution phase, the central concept is a test of hypotheses or product assumptions, and the product itself through the minimum viable product (MVP). Some critics of the lean movement raised their concerns suggesting that MVP implies launching an inferior product to do a quick and dirty test. However, the definition of

MVP must be understood as MDP, where 'D' stands for 'desirable' (Heitmann 2014) and means that customers must desire the MVP; otherwise, testing an inferior version of the product does not make sense. Therefore, a new concept to illustrate this combined suggestion would be a minimum viable product which is desirable at the same time (MVDP) which must be developed and tested. However, this concept, reported by Heitmann (2014), is an original concept from the Kano Model, where 'must be quality' cannot be compromised in the product development phase. Attractive quality becomes something you can manoeuvre through. Thanks to Kano's original conceptualization in the TQM movement, utilizing similar logic in the i4.0 era may prove the model's generalizability in a broader domain from products to service, and in many IT sectors' i4.0-related technologies, products, and services, enabled by these technological transformations.

Figure 3 uses an envelope of jobs-to-be-done theory (Christensen, Hall, Dillon, and Duncan 2016). In this theory, entrepreneurs must try to understand what the customer will do with the product or service they are going to develop during the early phase of venturing. In other words, customers are hiring the product to fulfil functional, psycho-social, or other related needs that they have. In the old paradigm of market research, most of the time, correlational attributes or characteristics of the products and customer's buying behaviour was used, which resulted in start-up failures. However, aiming to understand the broader jobs-to-be-done understanding by using the BMOL loop and customer development model, or, in a combined sense, a lean start-up, would be more beneficial than either/or philosophies. My underlying thesis is that these tools could be used as complementary, rather than competing, tools of philosophies.

Through the jobs-to-be-done theoretical lens, lean start-up becomes even more credible, but March's (1991) theory of exploration and exploitation drives the choices made by the entrepreneur in balancing these dichotomies. As the customer development model mainly focused on the attributes as correlational in the past, in my model, I have deliberately introduced customers' jobs-to-be-done perspectives in building causal links with the product's characteristics and experience around it. This paradigm change in thinking makes the model comprehensive and plausible, and takes away the luck component from the previously understood serendipity in entrepreneurial pursuits.

In acknowledging this, this book involved me in much research and in-depth digestion of the key giants' models in the entrepreneurial discourse.

However, decision modelling in Chapter 6 anchors another approach from causation, and introduces effectuation models as well. In causal models, we look for antecedents that explain the variance in the outcome variable entrepreneurial success. But in effectuation models, we orient ourselves through available means, adding resources, leveraging constraints, engaging stakeholders, and building experiments to understand the emerging future, using process-oriented research. Though most of the models are based on jobs-to-be-done thinking, in decision making, we combine both causation and effectuation thinking (Sarasvathy 2001).

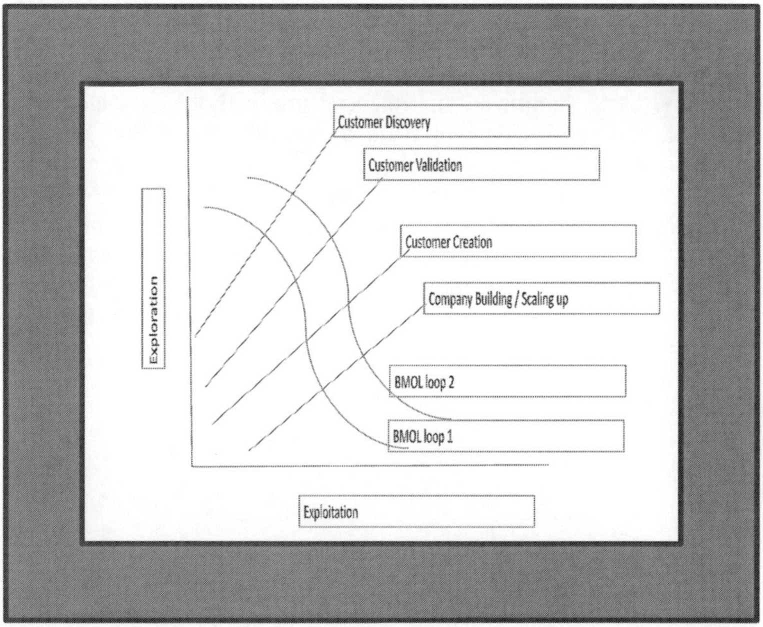


Figure 3-3. Entrepreneurial exploration and exploitation, BMOL loops, and Customer development model (adapted from Bhandari 2018)

**Industry 4.0 Business Model Canvas.** Apart from building on the existing literature of customer development, lean start-up, and agile thinking, this book's significant contribution lies in integrating the industry 4.0 enabled business model canvas (i4.0 BMC) in contrast to the normal business model canvas in entrepreneurial exploration and exploitation. As shown in Figure 4, there are 11 elements (9 in the earlier model) in the i4.0 BMC.

The central issue in the i4.0BMC is the unfair advantage and possibility of serving not only shareholders, but also society and the planet. In this notion, shareholders' supremacy is, albeit, challenged, and entrepreneurs are maximizing stakeholders' value in contrast to merely focusing on it thus making the sustainable development goals (SDGs) suggested by the United Nations a reality at a macro level. The latter part's full implementation may be the next book's agenda, but for now, these assumptions are optimized with CLV.

**The unfair advantage created by i4.0.** The future of innovation and platformization enabled by i4.0 technologies will have the following benefits: additional digital revenue; cost reduction; risk reduction; tailored or customized solutions; the possibility of incremental improvement on a real-time basis; optimization; enhanced productivity; foresight for a new product; and service development, and builds confidence. Summing all these together, if any players in the industry are not adapting to i4.0-related changes, they will only be found in history books. Managing the risk associated with capturing those listed values must be done in advance. Labour unrest due to layoffs created by automation and smart business models is one issue that the entrepreneur needs to plan to tackle in due course. Similarly, there are many regulatory changes which need to be made before fully utilizing the unfair advantages created by this digital revolution.

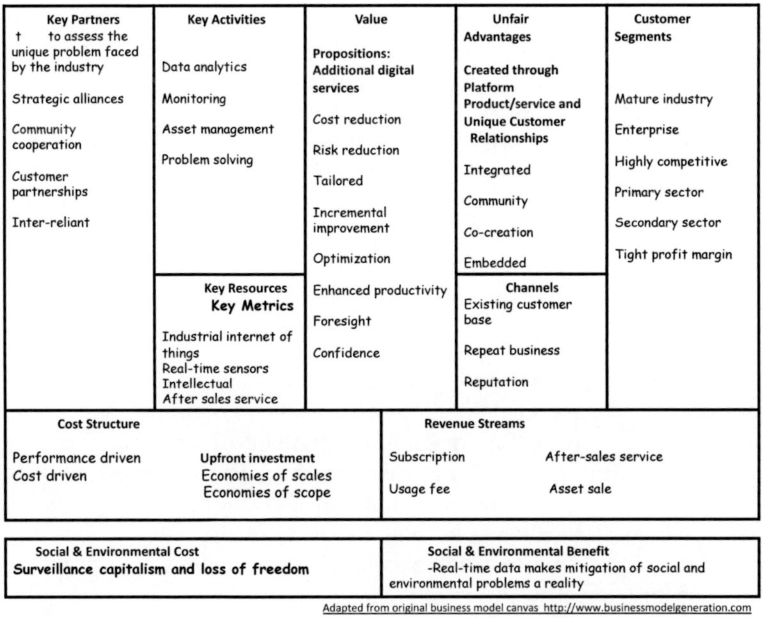


Figure 3-4. i4.0 Business Model Canvas (i4.0BMC) (Synthesized from Osterwalder 2010, Gierej 2017, Schaefer, Walker, and Flynn 2017, Maurya 2012, LAENSTACK).

The 11 elements of i4.0BMC are listed below, and shown in Figure 4, and a brief discussion about each component is presented below:

1. Key partners
2. Key activities
3. Key resources (metrics)
4. Value proposition
5. Unfair advantages
6. Customer segments
7. Channels
8. Cost structure
9. Revenue structure
10. Social and environmental costs
11. Social and environmental benefit

**Key Partners**. As the new wave will erase many silos inside the organization and across the organization's boundary, key partners will be the cornerstones of the generation of a new business model. These partnerships will be the value-added components to assess industry's unique problem, which could be solved through strategic alliances, as was shown by the airline industry. There can be a community of cooperation rather than competition. Porter's notion of competitive supremacy is being replaced by cooperative supremacy, where network power and network position determine value creation and capture alike. Ecosystem thinking drives start-ups from inception. A partnership, not only with suppliers and distributors, but also with customers, could herald a new wave of customer discovery, validation, and customer creation at the same time. Rather than self-reliance, the idea now is to build inter-reliance.

**Key Activities**. The new dimensions inside this block of i4.0BMC are mainly driven by data analytics to gather, analyse, optimize, and go for predictive models in decision making, rather than prescriptive models in the past. Monitoring and evaluation is something that becomes real-time and more efficient. Asset allocation and management in 5G technologies, sensors, or total architectures, become the need of the hour. Rather than waiting for a long time to resolve issues, a new approach to problem-solving becomes a reality.

**Key Resources/Key Metrics**. The significant change unfolding in front of any entrepreneur now revolves around the industrial Internet of Things (IIoT), real-time sensors with 5G-enabled data transmission links to cloud-based servers, intellectuals with data science, machine learning, and state of the art after-sales service. While entrepreneurs may think this might just be an evolution of existing IT, its impact in industries and start-ups is phenomenal. Let us not get blinded by the obvious, but be vigilant in understanding the implications of the unfair advantages firms are achieving due to i4.0 technologies and resources. With these metrics and data, the wisdom the decision-makers have, surpasses all other revenue streams. Data-as-a-service may become another frontier of the business model as well.

**Value Proposition/Additional Digital Services**. The i4.0-enabled business model reduces cost and risk, and helps build tailored solutions, empowers incremental improvement, has the power of optimization as discussed earlier in the BMOL loop, enhances productivity, builds foresight, and bolsters confidence. Though it sounds like a fairy-tale, these drive the unfair advantages discussed earlier.

**Channels**. For existing businesses, the existing customer base will be essential, but for new start-ups, customer discovery and customer validation assumptions are that, with the help of i4.0, entrepreneurs can build repeat business and reputation-based thinking in all MVP testing phases.

**Customer Segments**. Entrepreneurs have a high chance of transforming industry with their disruptive innovation where the industry is mature enough, and highly competitive with a tight profit margin.

**Cost Structure and Revenue Streams**. Although the cost structure will be performance-driven, upfront investments are needed to trigger the transformation project. The good side of such a transformation, innovation, or venture, is that subscription business models are feasible, usage-based fees could be charged, and after-sales service could be a revenue stream. In earlier transformation, IT only enabled cost efficiency, but in this new transformation, i4.0 enables new revenue and business model streams, which is why the world's best companies are fighting for a piece of the pie made out of such transformative technology and emerging business models.

**Social and Environmental Cost and Benefit**. In traditional business models, entrepreneurs needed to think about differentiation advantage or cost leadership, so that sustainable competitive advantage could be achieved. However, in the i4.0 era, the business model itself is built around the unfair advantages created by i4.0. Provided the entrepreneur finds the business model anchored in these unfair advantages, the business is sustainable in the long run, and competition becomes irrelevant.

Everyone is trying to create their 'blue ocean' where there is no cut-throat competition such as in the 'red ocean'. Creating one's own small street and becoming a monopolist in that street is far better than competing on a highway of multiple competitors for the same business model where profit is the main motive. This novelty makes the i4.0 BMC a unique contribution to synthesis from various authors' contributions, as listed in Figure 4. However, tools and technologies are neither good nor bad in themselves. How the user of the technology uses that technology rests on that user. In this perspective, society's morality keeps competition alive, as free and fair competition drives innovation, and progress must be safeguarded. Otherwise, the world will lose the slim hope of creative destruction suggested by Schumpeter, and the fundamental tenet of capitalism to correct itself becomes unfeasible.

As briefly outlined in the issues and controversies, using effectuation theory in making MVP decisions and pivot or persevere decisions after customer validation - the logic of control - can be used. As far as you can control the future outcome, you do not need to predict it. The future can be co-created in harmony with the environment, using a logic of how much you can afford to lose, rather than the expected return. Rather than focusing on the competitive advantages, an entrepreneur may build competitive models of strategic alliances and partnerships. Rather than exploiting the pre-existing knowledge to create the future, effectuation logic takes contingencies as given constraints and empowers entrepreneurs to leverage those contingencies. Therefore, as said earlier, the entrepreneurial notion needs to embrace control logic rather than a prediction of the future. Therefore, affordable loss, acceptable risk, strategic partnerships, and control logic, become four principles based on effectuation theory (Sarasvathy 2001).

In linking effectuation logic with entrepreneurial exploration and exploitation, entrepreneurs may think that decisions related to exploration activities must follow effectuation logic. In contrast, decisions related to exploitation-related activities must follow causation models. Thus, in balancing entrepreneurial exploration and exploitation, both effectuation and causation thinking can be utilized. Rather than looking at these dichotomies as either/or, entrepreneurs must embrace both approaches, and learn to balance these, as and when the environment and the issues at hand demand. While ambidexterity at the entrepreneurial level would be good, genetics have not contributed to shaping such outcomes in large numbers. Only a small percentage of the population falls within that breed of ambidextrous entrepreneurs. However, the models and data science available to entrepreneurs through the adoption of i4.0 may mitigate an entrepreneur's weaknesses so that the entrepreneurial level's ambidexterity can be realized. Though the implications of this will feature in a separate chapter at the end, it is vital to highlight critical implications of i4.0 research and implementation together with the impact on globalization, economic nationalism, or populism — the bubble we are witnessing in recent times, as triggered by BREXIT and 'Trumponomics'.

**Implications of i4.0 research and implementation**. Liao et al. (2017) is an excellent point to start discussing further research. As discussed earlier, to make i4.0 successful, following Liao et al.'s (2017) recommendations to go for horizontal integration, vertical integration, and end-to-end digital integration, must be realized. As the industry is just evolving, there are eight priority areas for action suggested by Liao et al. (2017). I concur with those recommendations, such as developing standardization and reference architecture, managing complex systems, delivering a comprehensive broadband infrastructure, and prioritizing safety and security. Similarly, a new innovative work organization and design, training and continuing professional development, regulatory framework, and resource productivity and efficiency, must all be taken seriously by the entrepreneur to realize the ubiquitous applications enabled by i4.0.

**Implications of i4.0 on globalization, economic nationalism or populism.** The exploration to understand how global companies could be established led to the international business (IB) literature, strategic adaptation literature, and competitive strategies literature. Surprisingly, the academic literature reported mixed findings, as discussed earlier, on the benefits of internationalization, which has implications for scaling i4.0 innovation in the global market. One school of thought suggests a diversification discount (Denis, Denis and Yost 2002), while another says globalization is beneficial due to the flexibility it creates (Chang, Kogut and Yang 2016).

For the last century, globalization has been seen as a bane and a boon at the same time. Globalization enabled economic integration, but at the same time, created political marginalization and cultural homogenization. Recent published articles in *The Economist* suggest that globalization is in retreat. Populists are using slogans such as "our country first" and "immigration is evil". Spreading these messages has been more straightforward than previously, thanks to Facebook and other media outlets. There is unease in the cultural realm. Per Professor Farooq Contractor, there is an emerging sense of "global consciousness" and sensitivity to noble thoughts, and fear and nationalism at the same time. Driven by this global phenomenon, this chapter takes a position at the corporate level to understand whether internationalization, or, for that matter, scaling a company as per a customer development model, is good for companies in the long run.

At this point in the history of time, this generation is witnessing a significant revolution triggered by AI, cloud computing, IoT, big data, and a new generation of mobile technologies. Even though there are opposing views on globalization, the Y-generation's collective conscience may be on the cusp of embracing openness. China is optimistically forging ahead with the One Belt, One Road initiative to connect China with Europe and Southeast Asia. Similarly, India welcomes FDI to leverage its demographic dividend with a young workforce ready for new challenges.

Levinthal and March (1993) argue that learning has many virtues. However, the learning process is far from perfect. In an organization, education has to balance trade-offs in developing new knowledge, exploring and exploiting current skills and capabilities. This inherent tension might be even higher in the case of i4.0, as disruption demands more exploration at the expense of exploitation. There are three forms of learning myopia; the tendency to overlook distant times, distant places, and failures. In simpler terms, short-termism or the 'success (or exploitation) trap' is too strong in modern management thinking driven by quarterly results and share price. Thus, managers need to build ambidextrous (both exploration and exploitation) competencies to survive in the long run. This has vast implications for entrepreneurial ventures in the era of i4.0. Learning from large firms and SMEs, start-ups may take a different approach, as small start-ups are not scaled-down versions of large firms. However, large companies' internationalization experiences when they were scaling up could provide better planning and experimentation perspectives for start-ups.

Further research in integrating design thinking into the early phase of business model search, and later phases of business model execution, could be exciting, as the current version does not connect design thinking with starting. Later in the detailed discussions about customer creation, we touched upon design thinking but not pervasively. Future research in integrating empathy into the customer discovery and validation phases already makes much sense. Technology-specific business models for each type of technology could be thought through, but combining all technologies' benefits under the i4.0 umbrella makes it more plausible. Further research challenging Porterian thought could be the next frontier of research. However, this school of thought has started to correct its books and papers with revised frameworks and philosophies, such as the customer shared value (CSV) approach. However, this doctrine may no longer be valid as a correction to the old models, but a substantially new approach to entrepreneurship is further due.

The recommendation suggested above could be possible by opting for a new dependent variable or measure of success. The IB literature and strategic management literature use return on assets (ROA) and Tobin's Q (market value/book value) or similar dependent variables based on accounting standards. ROA is the generally-used measure of success in the businesses where relentless pursuit of profit is the mantra. However, Tobin's Q is a better measure, as it has implications for the market taken into consideration. Even then, short-term myopia is dominant in the corporate world, basically driven by quarterly results and share price. To not fall prey to this myopia, one needs to focus on a new measure of success.

A recent publication by Nobel laureate Oliver Hart, and Luigi Zingales, proposes that *"Companies Should Maximize Shareholder Welfare Not Market Value*" (2017). This somehow challenges, albeit differently, the Milton Friedman doctrine of 1970: "[…] conduct the business by [shareholders'] desires, which generally will be to make as much money as possible while conforming to the basic rules of the society, both those embodied in law and those embodied in ethical custom". The question is, where is the morality in business? One of the future researches one should undertake would be to establish a precise link between moral philosophy, investment policy, and a prosocial investors' 'invest and engage' approach, as suggested by Hart and Zingales, and corporate policy.

The Principal-Agent theory mainly drives CEOs' honesty and attention. As per the theory, CEOs have been rewarded for maximizing shareholder's value. The majority of the stock-trading volume comes from institutional investors, such as hedge funds and pension funds. On average, they own the stock for a year or so. They are only exploiting the company in the short-term. They are not investing for the long run, as suggested by exploration orientation earlier. Capitalism needs to fix this conundrum before achieving success in establishing sustainable companies. CEOs must be rewarded for long-term company health, employee prosperity, and societal and environmental impact. A new dependent variable must be developed and practiced. Thus, I propose that a new dependent variable should measure success in terms of social influence, environmental return, and finally, economic return: 3PS (People, Planet, and Profit).

## CONCLUSION

The i4.0BMC as a guiding post in running BMOL loops in exploring and exploiting makes such a compelling and comprehensive framework; the power lies in the team's execution capacity. Yes, we need product leadership and operational excellence, but the solutions will falter without customer intimacy. Thus, using the assumptions in i4.0BMC as a testbed in understanding the customer, and the potential growth engine mainly assisted by the 'Optimization' block need to be considered. The power of i4.0BMC in creating unfair advantages from inception begs respect from every entrepreneur. Recognizing these hidden gems in i4.0BMC itself is worth remembering in building new ventures. Perhaps we are entering into an era where start-up failures due to premature scaling will be fewer and fewer, while balancing profitability and innovation becomes feasible. The unfair advantage created through integrated solutions, community participation, co-creation, and embeddedness of the answers, will drive the next wave of innovation and entrepreneurship alike.

The beauty of capitalism is that it creates its path to correct the course and sail again.

Globalization is not in retreat, or is it? However, it needs to correct itself for anomalies and forge ahead. Occupy Wall-Street movements and riots in front of G20 meetings are crying for change. While the World Economic Forum is busy with press releases, the World Social Forum is raising its concerns. Unless, and until, the concerned authority listens to these genuine voices, capitalism will falter. Choices are the symbols of the generation — respecting the other side of the table and building harmony where dignity, peace, and prosperity, can be possible in this lifetime. Celebrating 'global consciousness' must be the focus of the new generation.

The technological innovation in automation and efficiency innovation is taking away around 70% of jobs, and globalization the rest. This is creating abundant capital resulting in a capital cost close to zero. As suggested by Professor Christensen from Harvard, unless, and until, we invest in empowering innovation which creates jobs and uses capital, we are heading towards stagnation, as is evident in Japan over a long time. The United States is facing the same problem. Due to the onset of i4.0, new multinationals or meta-nationals will emerge, and benefit from this change should be policymaking's primary focus. Are we racing against machines, or we are co-opting machines to build a safer and freer world?

## REFERENCES

Atzori, L., Iera, A., and Morabito, G. (2010). The internet of things: A survey. *Computer networks*, *54*(15), 2787-2805.

Barney, J. (1991). Firm resources and sustained competitive advantage. *Journal of Management*, *17*(1), 99-120.

Baur, C., and Wee, D. (2015). Manufacturing's next act. *McKinsey Quarterly, Jun.*

Bhandari, K. (2017). *Internationalization and Organizational Ambidexterity for Sustainable Performance: Moderating Effects of Firm-specific*

*Advantages and Competitive Strategies*, Acta Wasaensia 379, Vaasan yliopisto, University of Vaasa.

Bhandari, K. R. (2018). Balancing Exploration and Exploitation through Customer Development Model: Leveraging Industry 4.0 for Sustainable Performance. In *Analyzing the Impacts of Industry 4.0 in Modern Business Environments* (pp. 147-160). IGI Global.

Blank, S. (2013). *The four steps to the epiphany: successful strategies for products that win*. BookBaby.

Bughin, J., Chui, M., and Manyika, J. (2015). An executive's guide to the Internet of Things. *McKinsey Quarterly*.

Chang, S., Kogut, B., and Yang, J. S. (2016). Global diversification discount and its discontents: A bit of self-selection makes a world of difference. *Strategic Management Journal*, *37*(11), 2254-2274.

Christensen, C. M., Hall, T., Dillon, K., and Duncan, D. S. (2016). Know your customers' jobs to be done. *Harvard Business Review*, *94*(9), 54-62.

Denis, D. J., Denis, D. K., and Yost, K. (2002). Global diversification, industrial diversification, and firm value. *The Journal of Finance*, *57*(5), 1951-1979.

Gabrielsson, M., Seppälä, T., and Gabrielsson, P. (2016). Realizing a hybrid competitive strategy and achieving superior financial performance while internationalizing in the high-technology market. *Industrial Marketing Management*, *54*, 141-153.

Gierej, S. (2017). The framework of a business model in the context of the Industrial Internet of Things. *Procedia Engineering*, *182*(2017), 206-212.

Hart, O., and Zingales, L. (2017). Companies Should Maximize Shareholder Welfare Not Market Value.

Heitmann, J. (2014). *The Lean Start-up-A pragmatic view on its Flaws and Pitfalls* (Bachelor's thesis, University of Twente).

Karhu, K., Gustafsson, R., and Lyytinen, K. (2018). Exploiting and defending open digital platforms with boundary resources: Android's five platform forks. *Information Systems Research*, *29*(2), 479-497.

Kim, G., and Huh, M. G. (2015). Exploration and organizational longevity: The moderating role of strategy and environment. *Asia Pacific Journal of Management*, *32*(2), 389-414.

Lasi, H., Fettke, P., Kemper, H. G., Feld, T., and Hoffmann, M. (2014). Industry 4.0. *Business and Information Systems Engineering*, *6*(4), 239-242.

Lavie, D. (2006). The competitive advantage of interconnected firms: An extension of the resource-based view. *Academy of management review, 31*(3), 638-658.

Levinthal, D. A., and March, J. G. (1993). The myopia of learning. Strategic management journal, 14(S2), 95-112.

Liao, Y., Deschamps, F., Loures, E. D. F. R., and Ramos, L. F. P. (2017). Past, present, and future of Industry 4.0-a a systematic literature review and research agenda proposal. *International Journal of Production Research*, *55*(12), 3609-3629.

March, J. G. (1991). Exploration and exploitation in organizational learning. *Organization Science*, *2*(1), 71-87.

Marr, B. (June 20, 2016). What Everyone Must Know About Industry 4.0. *Forbes Magazine.* Accessed on 31.07.2017 from https://www.forbes.com/sites/bernardmarr/2016/06/20/what-everyone-must-know-about-industry-4-0/#5ed8a614795f

Maurya, A. (2012). Why Lean Canvas vs. Business Model Canvas? Leanstack.

Mazzei, M. J., and Noble, D. (2017). Big data dreams: A framework for corporate strategy. *Business Horizons*, *60*(3), 405-414.

Ocasio, W. (1997). Towards an attention-based view of the firm. *Strategic management journal*, 187-206.

Osterwalder, A., and Pigneur, Y. (2010). Business model canvas. *Self-published. Last*.

Penrose, E. T. (1959). The theory of the growth of the firm. *New York: Sharpe*.

Porter, M. E., and Advantage, C. (1985). Creating and Sustaining Superior Performance.

Porter, M. E., and Heppelmann, J. E. (2015). How smart, connected products are transforming companies. *Harvard Business Review*, *93*(10), 96-114.

Ries, E. (2011). *The lean startup: How today's entrepreneurs use continuous innovation to create radically successful businesses*. Crown Books.

Schaefer, D., Walker, J., and Flynn, J. (2017, August). A data-driven business model framework for value capture in Industry 4.0. In *Advances in Manufacturing Technology XXXI: Proceedings of the 15th International Conference on Manufacturing Research, Incorporating the 32nd National Conference on Manufacturing Research, September 5–7, 2017, University of Greenwich, UK* (Vol. 6, p. 245). IOS Press.

Spanos, Y. E., Zaralis, G., and Lioukas, S. (2004). Strategy and industry effects on profitability: evidence from Greece. *Strategic management journal*, *25*(2), 139-165.

Strange, R., Strange, R., Zucchella, A., and Zucchella, A. (2017). Industry 4.0, global value chains, and international business. *Multinational Business Review*, *25*(3), 174-184.

Teece, D. J. (2007). Explicating dynamic capabilities: the nature and microfoundations of (sustainable) enterprise performance. *Strategic management journal*, *28*(13), 1319-1350.

Teece, D. J. (2014). A dynamic capabilities-based entrepreneurial theory of the multinational enterprise. *Journal of International Business Studies*, *45*(1), 8-37.

Teece, D. J. (2018). Business models and dynamic capabilities. *Long Range Planning*, *51*(1), 40-49.

Teece, D. J., Pisano, G., and Shuen, A. (1997). Dynamic capabilities and strategic management. *Strategic management journal*, 509-533.

Uotila, J., Maula, M., Keil, T., and Zahra, S. A. (2009). Exploration, exploitation, and financial performance: analysis of SandP 500 corporations. *Strategic Management Journal*, *30*(2), 221-231.

Vuori, T. O., and Huy, Q. N. (2016). Distributed attention and shared emotions in the innovation process: How Nokia lost the smartphone battle. Administrative Science Quarterly, 61(1), 9-51.

Wade, M., and Hulland, J. (2004). The resource-based view and information systems research: Review, extension, and suggestions for future research. *MIS Quarterly*, *28*(1), 107-142.

## KEY TERMS AND DEFINITIONS

**Entrepreneurial exploration:** Activities carried out as searching for innovation and future revenue sources.

**Entrepreneurial exploitation:** Activities carried out as maximizing current profit without thinking about future revenue sources when the current market saturates.

**Customer development model:** It has two parts: business model search and business model execution.

**BMOL loop:** Build-measure-optimize-learn loop where progress is validated learning for next iteration or future product decision.

**MVDP:** Minimum viable but desirable product at the same time. This is the new, improved conceptualization of the original minimum viable product (MVP), which gave a connotation that quality is compromised in testing the quick and dirty version of the product or service. However, as suggested by Kano's model, "must-be" qualities cannot be compromised even in MVP, for which scholars suggested a new concept of 'desirable' by the customers.

**i4.0BMC:** Industry 4.0 Business Model Canvas. This is the new, improved conceptualization of the original Business Model Canvas (BMC), which was useful but not comprehensive in capturing the details of i4.0 changes. From the older version's nine blocks, the improved performance has 11 blocks now. Creating unfair advantage becomes one of the primary key concepts inside the i4.0BMC.

# CHAPTER 4

# ENTREPRENEURIAL EXPLORATION AND EXPLOITATION: BUSINESS MODEL SEARCH PHASE I

**ABSTRACT**

*As i4.0 takes off, entrepreneurial exploration and exploitation in the business model search phases can be divided into customer discovery and customer validation phases; however, the guiding theory of jobs-to-be-done says that understanding multiple use cases is a must. The customer discovery phase demands knowledge of the changing locus of innovation and platform economics. This chapter's focus is to link open innovation and platformization in the presence of contingency variables on the potential future firm performance estimated as customer lifetime value (CLV). However, the real measure of progress in this phase is validated learning through the multiple iterations of open innovation activities, and platformization efforts inflated or deflated by contingencies in understanding jobs-to-be-done by the customer. Once the customer discovery phase validates some of the assumptions or hypotheses through BMOL testing and measuring the data based on the experiments, the second phase of business model search, called the customer validation phase starts. In the discovery phase, which is the focus of this chapter, all the interviews and observations are done in all blocks of i4.0BMC to test it in a minimum viable and desirable product (MVDP) or minimum viable concept (MVC), to understand the more significant product or solution that has a causal link with the jobs-to-be-done by the customer. Such MVDP or MVC reduces the cost of development and failure costs and can compete against luck, as Christensen et al. (2016) suggested. Once the learning in this phrase indicates that the product is feasible, only then does full prototype or pilot testing of the product start.*

Keywords: Customer discovery, Customer validation, Entrepreneurial exploration, Entrepreneurial exploitation, MVP, i4.0BMC,

## INTRODUCTION

The recent developments triggered by technological change's accelerated pace, famously labelled as Industry 4.0 (i4.0), is becoming a new economic and social force. A new paradigm is emerging where old business models are being transformed. Strategies are becoming real-time and fact-based, and new processes based on optimization algorithms are taking place. Bughin, Chui, and Manyika (2015) argued that the competition's primary differentiating factor would come from the Internet of Things (IoT). This changing landscape in competitive strategies triggered by the IoT and in general, from Industry 4.0 (i4.0), demands that senior leaders and board members think at the system level to solve the technological disruption's challenges. The opportunities are many, but gathering data together from different IoT systems may not be enough. This triggers analytical challenges for which developing or purchasing, customizing, and then deploying analytical software to get insights for decision-making, is highly important. IoT-enabled new business models would be the norm, rather than the exception.

Key terms used in this book are jobs-to-be-done, exploration, exploitation, i4.0, customer development model, and build-measure-optimize-learn (BMOL) loop. Jobs-to-be-done means using the product or service by the customer that enables them to buy the product. Exploration is defined as activities related to search, experiment, explore, innovate and aspire. This is good for the long-term, but the detrimental short-term as a perpetual search trap leads to firms' failure. Exploitation is defined as activities related to efficiency, productivity, and optimization. This is good for the short term, but bad for the long term, as the success trap leads to firms' failure (March 1991). Loosely defined, i4.0 is an umbrella concept where the Internet of Things, automation, cloud computing, 3D printing, digitalization, and mobile technologies enable new business models and drive innovation and efficiency. Blank (2013) noted that the customer development model has four phases: customer discovery, customer validation, customer creation, and company development.

Based on the *McKinsey Quarterly* paper, Industry 4.0 has become more than just a famous discourse in the manufacturing sector (Baur and Wee 2015). There is a growing convergence of trends and technologies with the potential to change the manufacturing landscape. Executives have started to understand that it is not mere hype, as it reveals the power of disruption in the way factories work. Some authors have called it the next industrial revolution. Thus, executives must embrace this change and plan for actions to sail the ship in the right direction. This could be achieved by learning new possibilities and exploiting the certainties in the current realities. March (1991) coined the term 'balancing exploration and exploitation' for a winning mindset.

The latest systematic literature review by Liao, Deschamps, Loures, and Ramos (2017) on the fourth industrial revolution suggested that the top 5 keyword clusters are emerging in the existing literature as: industry 4.0; cyber-physical systems' manufacturing; smart factory; and the Internet of Things. This disruption will enable horizontal integration, vertical integration, and end-to-end digital integration. Amidst the buzz around i4.0, there is a lack of understanding of managing such an uncertainty. This paper attempts to solve that puzzle by bringing a proven theoretical construct from the academic literature and merging it with the recent development in entrepreneurial ventures. Earlier, these concepts were used in startups, but with General Electric introducing them within their organizations, they became a mainstream agenda.

As they progress in i4.0 technologies, which include 5G-enabled solutions, humankind is also on the cusp of mega changes in the status quo. This new wave not only paves the way for new innovation, but also enables a new wave of platformization. The locus of innovation crosses the firm and even industry boundaries, while value creation and value capture are happening at the firm's periphery or industry. Earlier models of innovation and value creation or value capture are no more valid. Due to digitalization, even manufacturing companies are riding the servitization wave to bundle services into the product.

Moogk (2012) applied MVDP in his research to understand the resource crunch which entrepreneurs face in their quest to change the world through new technology and its commercial application. lean start-up is now universally applicable in all sizes of company. Under resource constraints and extreme uncertainty, and the pressure to make efficient use of resources to build a useful product in the long run, MVDP is used to test whether the product's value to customers, and the entrepreneurs' expectations of growth, are feasible. Such testing is done through experimentation, which evaluates the product's value proposition, unfair advantages, and other elements of i4.0BMC. Later on, the same approach could be used with the right metrics for three distinct growth types, of which discussion will be made in the solutions and recommendation section in this chapter. Under conditions of uncertainty, facts are scarce. The only way is to learn is through experimentation, which gives accelerated learning, to reduce the uncertainty of commercialization and time needed to serve the market faster.

## BACKGROUND

As is evident from the wave of development in automation, robotics, AI, cloud computing, 3D printing, synthetic biology, medicine, nanomaterials, 5G, and other related technologies, and as discussed in Chapter 3 under theoretical models, Optimization loops will enable a new wave of machine learning and algorithms; humans are racing against machines, and machines are seeking to overcome the capacity of humans - called a singularity. Araya (2013) interviewed serial entrepreneur Vivek Wadhwa, who, rightly, calls these technologies exponential ones. Silicon Valley now boasts the Singularity University, where future leaders in harnessing these exponential technologies are being developed. Perhaps in 10-20 years, these technologies will solve significant challenges to get out of the garage and make an impact in an unprecedented way. Piketty's (2020) vision is to have a real sense of freedom and a vibrant capitalist society where justice prevails for all, with a narrow scope of any inequality regime (Piketty 2020). While everything seems interesting in Piketty's narratives, participatory social democracy is not enough for me, as I believe in entrepreneurial exploration and exploitation as a cornerstone of building ethical, just, and moral capitalism, where Schumpeterian creative destruction is the norm rather than the exception; Sen's justice prevails to all, and environment does not bleed its pain with coronaviruses where the mass extinction of the species is being seen as a challenge to human civilization. There are three general questions explored in this chapter. First, how to avoid the success, or perpetual search, trap. Second, how can the firm leverage the customer development model for the innovation triggered by i4.0? Third, how to accelerate the pace of innovation in i4.0.

**How to avoid a success trap.** Bhandari's latest dissertation (2017) provides a plausible solution for an 'Innovator's Dilemma', presented in a groundbreaking book by Harvard University Professor, Clayton Christensen. Firms should be 'ambidextrous' in reaping short-term profits, (called exploitation), and innovating for long-term success, (called exploration), at the same time. If the relative ratio between exploration and exploitation is in the very low range or very high range, it is not beneficial. However, gaining an optimum range in the middle helps firms to avoid the success trap, or for that matter, the exploitation trap. Such a trap exists due to the relentless pursuit of profits (e.g. Nokia) at the expense of innovation and experimentation for new products and services.

However, there are perpetual search traps as well. Xerox was once in this trap. However, following overall cost leadership did not impact exploration and exploitation, but differentiation and hybrid strategies were necessary. Thus, in the i4.0 era, a firm's attention towards what is emerging in the long term, and what could be exploited for short-term profit, is even greater than before. As discussed earlier, i4.0 is a different phenomenon, as it will enable new business models and change the competitive landscape completely. In this transformation, the ecosystem and the platform-based economy are at the forefront. Earlier knowledge and skills would not be sufficient as they demand the understanding of new technologies and software which drives the innovation.

**How to accelerate the pace of innovation in i4.0.** It took forty years to understand the hybrid strategies in strategic management literature, as evident from the literature. Over 50 years of research in international business (IB) literature has been blinded by the obvious. It has mixed findings on how to resolve a fundamental internationalization question: how to scale up a venture in uncertain conditions. The extant literature for fifty years has been inconclusive. Based on the latest literature, rather than using multiple theories, it is good to focus on the dynamic capabilities-based view (DCV) (Teece et al. 1997, Teece 2007, 2014) to streamline the theoretical contribution. However, dynamic capabilities are dynamic by nature, and tracing them in innovation and scaling activities is exceptionally challenging. Another implication of that earlier realization was that the resource-based view (RBV) (1991) and DCV are siblings. However, recent understanding after immersion into the theoretical framework and operationalization, is that the resource position barrier as advocated by the RBV needs to be leveraged to realize the sense, and seize, and orchestrate the notion of DCV. Entrepreneurial management and empowering innovations are only possible from the DCV perspective. The scaling of innovation under extreme uncertainty created by i4.0 moves from advantage-seeking mode to opportunity-seeking mode. Explaining the firm-specific advantages would be more comfortable from the DCV perspective as well. Thus, a clear theoretical rationale for navigating the business model generated by i4.0, and the discussions in this chapter, is DCV.

While academicians struggle to provide a solution to the puzzle of entrepreneurial exploration and exploitation and the balance thereof, Harvard University academicians, however, silently, gave plausible hope already in 2005 in their seminal piece "Marketing Malpractice" (Christensen, Cook, and Hall 2005). The theory of jobs-to-be-done (the underlying idea of this book) was outlined in this piece, but did not gain popularity until 2016, with the publication "Know your customers' jobs to be done" (Christensen, Hall, Dillon, and Duncan 2016). In these sequels, understanding the customer use cases of a product or service under development, and figuring out causal (no correlation) attributes of buying decisions by the customer, has been hailed as a breakthrough idea ("Competing Against Luck", Hall, Christensen, Dillon, and Duncan 2016). Throwing a dice for millions of dollars in the hope of breakthrough innovations and disruptions is a thing of the past, but still, there is a long way to go. Hope rises from the advent of i4.0 and the real-time optimization loops in understanding the causal links between jobs-to-be-done and customers' buying decisions for the product or service in the discussion.

The emerging literature in i4.0 focuses on global value chains and international business (Strange, Strange, Zucchella and Zucchella 2017). This emerging worldview tracks the widespread adoption of new digital technologies, such as the Internet of Things, big data and analytics, robotic systems, and additive manufacturing. One of the essential aspects of this phenomenon is to see the impact on the location and organization of activities within the global value chains (GVCs). Studying these implications for GVCs, the exciting part explores how these emerging technologies create new configurations involving suppliers, firms, and customers. For this to be successful, Teece (2014) argued that recombination of resources and capabilities is essential. Concurring with this, Strange, Strange, Zucchella, and Zucchella (2017) found that the i4.0-related technologies are on the cusp of disrupting how and where activities are located and organized within GVCs. The goal is not only disruption, but to figure out who captures the value created within those GVCs. Implications for strategy to ensure that the company can grab the value created by this disruption are huge. A new competitor may come entirely from a new industry, as digitalization has enabled many conglomerates such as FANG (Facebook, Apple, Netflix, and Google). However, to safeguard against the cyber-risks and implications for individuals' privacy, extra attention to security must be paid. This means regulation is just lagging with the pace of change.

The research frontier calling for researchers is still in its infancy. A new innovative business model, efficiency projects, and implications for the theory and research of management are on the verge of emerging. We need to understand the relationships between business model alternatives, competitive strategy, and the resulting performance outcomes in the new industrial internet wave (Burmeister et al. 2016). While I am teaching, I use straightforward existing communication channels like Facebook Messenger to communicate with students (customers). Almost real-time communication has enhanced learning skills and customer satisfaction levels and helped build brand ambassadors for the University.

Imagine the future classroom, with online learning materials, and connected universities, delivering a new experience to the classroom, and learning solutions, in real-time. If this is happening in the service sector, sensor-enabled products' power will revolutionize the customer experience — even though we need to fix privacy issues at its core. Changes in distribution channels and customer relations, empowered by bots and AI, will be the new frontier in understanding the customer better and saving costs simultaneously. Burmeister et al. (2016) argued that the concept of B2B is changing into B2B2C, as manufacturers are getting live data from smart products directly, and new platform business is knocking on the doors of customers already. For companies, embracing the open business model suggested by Chesbrough (2006) might be a good strategy as networks and platforms with blurred boundaries will be a new reality.

Lean start-up (Ries 2011) was developed through the concept of Toyota's lean production system. According to Ries (2011),

> "A start-up is a human institution designed to create a new product or service under conditions of extreme uncertainty".

The conditions of extreme uncertainty make the concept of MV*D*P even more critical in the startup world, but the large corporations are equally facing the changes in all spheres - political, economic, socio-cultural, technological, environmental, and global forces (PESTLEG). Such PESTLEG-enabled changes are forcing everyone to think like a startup. For any startup dealing with an unknown problem and unknown solutions in the future, MV*D*P as an experimentation concept is an exciting approach.

The old paradigm of entrepreneurship normally builds a full product over a long period. It launches into the market to realize that the entrepreneurs' vision is a hallucination rather than a reality. In contrast to the old paradigm of spending enormous resources and failing (9 out of 10), lean start-up tests the product in smaller concepts, and tests the right growth engine using smaller expenses, to scale it up and succeed later in a full production stage. As suggested by BMOL, a faster learning loop is highly recommended to fend off competitors through excellence in building product leadership and customer intimacy.

## OPEN INNOVATION AND PLATFORMIZATION

### Issues, Controversies, Problems

A practical solution to understand the underlying puzzle triggered by i4.0 is to create a map of the balancing of exploration and exploitation with the customer development model and the role of lean start-up thinking mainly represented by the build-measure-optimization-learn (BM*O*L) loop discussed in Chapter 3.

### Balancing exploration and exploitation in the age of i4.0

Based on the author's early career at Nokia and its evolution, the motivation to explore what makes a firm sustainable in the long run has been the focus of the research. While at Nokia, the focus was on exploiting the GSM technology to the fullest extent, but the exploration and, for that matter, exploitation, of the fast-emerging 3G innovation, was missing. However, by then, the firm was also good at the exploration of new technologies. Reading emails was possible in Nokia Communicator, long before Apple's touchscreen iPhone. After a few years, it was visible that Nokia had missed the most significant disruption in the mobile industry, and Nokia Mobile Phones had to be sold. So, this raised a question, why do giants fail? Or, in other words, what makes a company successful in the long-run? – the broader research question of this chapter. However, this chapter's scope has been limited to the key antecedents and moderating variables of sustainable performance in the age of i4.0.

March (1991) suggested that balancing the exploration and exploitation trade-off is crucial to succeeding in the long run. Exploration implies search, experimentation, development, and innovation-related activities that have a performance impact in the long run. If a firm is geared towards short-term financial gains indicated by its stock price, it does not invest in exploration activities. This results in an exploitation (or success) trap, or learning myopia. The balancing act of exploration and exploitation results in multiple business model innovations. There are two performance curves depending on what type of build-measure-learn (BMOL) loop (Ries 2011) capability the firm has. At a weaker BMOL loop of execution, the balance curve is lower, while at a more robust BML loop, the performance curve is higher. For i4.0 related innovation, the breakthrough is usually in changing the business model. Therefore, understanding the relative exploration measured as the ratio of exploration divided by the sum of exploration and exploitation would be an attractive index to understand the balance of exploration and exploitation.

Wade and Hulland (2004) assessed the RBV and information systems research. Their assessment of information technology's effects on firm performance found mixed results (see Table 5, page 125 for more details). A large body of researchers saw a direct and positive impact on firm performance, while Warner (1987) was the only study reporting a negative impact. According to Wade and Hulland (2004), the RBV treats information assets and systems differently. "The former is asset-based, while the latter comprises a mixture of assets and capabilities formed around the productive use of information technology. We contend that the RBV, through its focus on attributes and its recognition of the importance of resource complementarity, will uncover an enhanced role for information systems in sustained firm competitiveness" (Wade and Hulland 2004 132). Thus, following the similar tone and view of digitalization, this chapter's focus is to reconcile these mixed findings. One of the significant aspects of digitalization is driven by big data. According to Mazzei and Noble (2017), there are three tiers of the impact of big data. First, big data could be just a tool in the traditional value chain. Second, big data could be a stimulus for new ventures and industry development. The third tier argues for big data as a driver of competitive strategy. As is evident in this discussion, anchored in the RBT and organizational learning perspectives, the expected relationship between digitalization and long-term performance is curvilinear.

As discussed in Wade and Hulland (2004), a few authors found that the information system (IS) has no effect on performance, but a large majority of authors suggested that there are contingent effects of other constructs, such as top managements' commitment to IS. Attention is a sacred resource, and as per Ocasio (1997), studying the RBV in tandem with the attention-based view (ABV) is the right approach for sustainable competitive advantage. However, this chapter does not elaborate on the ABV as such, to limit the scope.

**Business Model Innovation Process.** In the past, my own experience in the multinational and start-up world infers that the business model innovation (BMI) process generally resides with the product development department or team. The changing reality of i4.0-triggered innovation is not restricted only to the single product level or department. This demands the BMI process must be run at the CEO or top management team level, as it crosses all boundaries (inside or outside) and needs partnerships and alliances, moving away from competitive supremacy to competitive supremacy where all stakeholders are respected and 'customer shared value' (CSV) (Porter and Kramer 2019) is possible. The idea behind the separation of business model innovation and product development is based on the logic that traditional product development processes follow stage-gate processes. BMI in the new era needs to follow agile, lean start-up, customer development, iteration, scrum design thinking, and hypothesis-based development. This demands flexibility and market-relatedness, experimentation, learning, and optimization loops (Burmeister et al. 2016).

During the customer discovery interview process, all assumptions based on i4.0BMC components must be digested and understood before developing the MV*D*P. Once MV*D*P is tested, and proper validated learning is achieved, then the choice as to whether to go for decision analysis based on Chapter 5 should be initiated. However, until then, 'must-be qualities', as suggested by Kano's model, must be met in the MVDP itself. Improving on the old MVP and embedding MV*D*P into the new conceptualization makes lean not only mean, but a quality assurance tool as well. Many entrepreneurs get the message wrong when they hear the word 'lean'. However, with the addition of desirable quality, the model will gain its credibility.

## SOLUTIONS AND RECOMMENDATIONS

**Jobs-to-be-done theory**. As discussed in the context of the larger framework, the BMOL loop finally gets its guiding idea to solve the jobs-to-be-done by customers, or various use cases and storyboards related to scenario testing. In this core process, in earlier notions, more correlational attributes were collected. Still, now with Christensen et al.'s (2016) approach, a causal link between the product or service and customers' buying behaviour is identified. This tool provides a strong foundation so that competing against luck, as outlined by Hall, Christensen, Dillon, and Duncan (2016) becomes finally feasible. According to the authors, it is more a matter of understanding customers' choices, and their behavior in making purchase decisions. This removes correlation in the process and builds causality in the real sense.

Using a guiding theory like jobs-to-be-done makes the next phase of the entrepreneurial wave far more exciting, while embedding it into the lean start-up concepts. However, with the theory's umbrella concept, the whole of lean testing and development gets a new meaning and hypotheses —

building causality into the system from correlational attributes of customers' buying behaviour.

Nambisan, Siegel, and Kenney (2018) touch on an essential aspect through which i4.0 technologies may enable companies to grasp open innovation and platformization. Both phenomena are reasonably new to the business world but have massive power in transforming entrepreneurial exploration and exploitation at the discovery phase of understanding the customer, as shown in Figure 1. This is the evidence that innovation is shifting towards more open and distributed models, and value creation and delivery are shifting towards the firm's boundaries, which makes the platform a norm rather than an exception. Figure 1 shows a model of optimizing CLV by embracing open innovation and platformization. However, in this model, we need to pay attention to contingencies such as digitization, institutional arrangements, entrepreneurial capabilities, regulation, and globalization, and entrepreneurship. As the phenomenon emerges, so does our understanding and the opportunity to build entrepreneurial exploration and exploitation models. Though the optimization variable seen in the figure is CLV, the primary unit of progress in this stage is validated learning. Learning from each iteration of idea generation and empathy-driven assessment by applying design thinking is the best approach in discovering customers. However, this process is better than in lean start-up concepts. Now the products are smart themselves, the business model is changing in many industries, and the imperative for future growth is optimized when we speak on a real-time basis.

**Open Innovation**. Open innovation is the use of purposive inflows and outflows of knowledge to accelerate internal innovation that triggers the emergence of a new era. It has great potential if we can race alongside the machine, rather than against it. The fear of joblessness, automation, efficiency, and the implications for industrial unrest, may be real for the short term, but the benefits created by this transformation are so huge, we should not be restricted to a pessimistic view. We must embrace the opportunities, building strengths in lean transformation capabilities, while preparing for threats and minimizing weaknesses.

**Platformization**. The value chain is being transformed as innovation and collaboration are best triggered by new waves of i4.0 technologies. This transformation is characterized as platformization in this book. However, managing proprietary and shared platforms is a daunting task.

Nambisan et al. (2018) posit an essential point on how open innovation and platformization have made entrepreneurship easy at some level, but an exploitation machine on the next level. Yes, it is enabling grassroots innovation, and new breeds of entrepreneurs are emerging, but at the mercy of platform providers on entrepreneurs' decision-making, strategies, and success. The platform providers have sole ownership of the critical issues such as how much to tax the income of entrepreneurs (Apple takes 30% of revenue from App Store). They decide on whether the solution provided by the entrepreneur is good enough or not and decide unilaterally on many issues which are mutual in nature. However, let us suppose we capture the value created by open innovation and platformization by building new models on managing pitfalls which I just suggested. In that case, we are on a firm footing to build an environment where efficiency and innovation must not be a trade-off. If we look across the common themes of platform companies, such as Uber, Airbnb, Alibaba, and Oyo, the following items emerge as underlying themes of building the platform business:

1. Technology,
2. Looking across the value chain,
3. Connectivity,
4. The convenience of the consumer factor (there is no substitute for that),
5. The entrepreneurial dream,

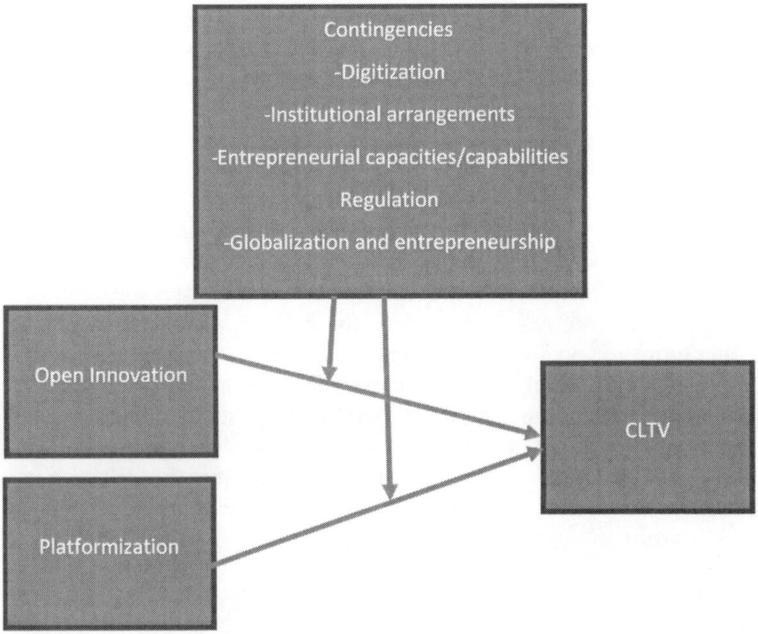


Figure 4-1 Open innovation, platformization and contingencies in entrepreneurial exploration and exploitation (Source: Inspired by Nambisan, Siegel, and Kenney 2018)

Elaborate discussion of the customer development model will be carried out in Chapter 5, but here it is good to understand that there are four phases inside the model: customer discovery, customer validation, customer creation, and scaling up. After the validation phase, pivot or persevere decisions are critical for a venture's success or failure. In much of my experience of mentoring to entrepreneurs, I have used the bubble chart in assessing the opportunity at the customer discovery phase, as shown in Figure 2, supported by Figure 3. With the help of Figure 3, we develop the likelihood of the occurrence of opportunities and potential. Multiplying both would give the opportunity level, which can be plotted on the bubble chart. The more gigantic the bubble, the better the opportunity, and vice-versa. Similar plotting could be done for the customer validation phase also, but in the customer validation phase, the idea is to run BMOL loops as fast as possible to test the value proposition and growth hypothesis at the same time.

Emerging start-up literature questions the old paradigm of developing fully-fledged products based on the entrepreneur's vision and raises concerns about dealing with unknowns in the future. The entrepreneur needs to understand the product's value or service, and the growth hypothesis to be tested. However, in i4.0BMC, one needs to make sure that optimization loops run faster, or, if possible, on a real-time basis. This makes the decision cycles quicker and testing all value hypotheses and growth hypotheses becomes a fruitful exercise. Under the assumption for growth, SVP (Sticky, Viral, and Paid) decisions are crucial, and all three must be tested. In such testing, the right measures or metrics must be used. Accounting-based metrics do not serve the purpose of understanding the value and growth hypotheses. For example, AARRR (Attention, Acquisition, Retention, Revenue, and Referral) cohort metrics would be a plausible approach, elaborated in the solutions section later. Ries (2011) even called for the removal of old accounting metrics, naming it vanity metrics. However, we are not against accounting measures, but instead we introduce CLV into the dependent or outcome variable, rather than ROA or ROS or profit as a metric.

Based on Schaefer, Walker, and Flynn (2017), data-driven business models will be a new norm rather than an exception. Such business models have created new market segments, economies of scale, and barriers to entry. Indeed, there are weaknesses and threats for which alertness is recommended while creating SO strategies for the future, where new i4.0 BMC is optimized through real-time algorithm-based AI, and cloud-computing solutions where platformization and open innovation are the norm rather than the exception.

As elaborated in Chapter 3 under the theoretical model, the new business model search ultimately tests all the assumptions in all 11 blocks of the business model canvas. It optimizes all cost and revenue parameters, keeping in view the social and environmental costs and benefits.

**Cost Structure and Revenue Streams**. Although the cost structure will be performance-driven, there are upfront investments needed to trigger the transformation project. The right side of such a transformation, innovation, or venture is that subscription business models are feasible, a usage-based fee could be charged, and after-sales service can be a revenue stream as well. In earlier transformation, IT only enabled cost efficiency, but in this new transformation, i4.0 enables new revenue and business model streams, which is why the world's best companies are fighting over a pie made out of such transformative technology and emerging business models.

**Social and Environmental Cost and Benefit**. In traditional business models, entrepreneurs needed to think for differentiation advantage or cost leadership so that sustainable competitive advantage could be achieved. However, in the i4.0 era, the business model itself is built around the unfair advantages created by i4.0. Provided the entrepreneur finds the business model anchored in these unfair advantages, the business is sustainable in the long run, and competition becomes irrelevant.

Everyone is trying to create their 'blue ocean' where there is no cut-throat competition in the 'red' sea. Creating a small street and becoming a monopolist in that street is far better than competing on a highway of multiple competitors for the same business model where profit is the main motive. This novelty makes the i4.0 BMC a unique contribution to synthesis from various authors' contributions, as listed in Figure 4.

Tools and technologies are neither good nor bad in themselves. How the user of the technology uses it, rests with that user. In this perspective, society's morality keeps competition alive, as free and fair competition drives innovation, and progress must be safeguarded. Otherwise, the world will lose the slim hope of creative destruction suggested by Schumpeter, and the real tenets for capitalism to correct itself become unfeasible. As briefly outlined in the issues and controversies, using effectuation theory in making MVP decisions and pivot or persevere decisions after customer validation allows the logic of control to be used. As far as you can control the future outcome, you do not need to predict it. You co-create the future in harmony with the environment with a logic based on how much you can afford to lose, rather than the expected return. Rather than focusing on the competitive advantages, an entrepreneur may build competitive models of strategic alliances and partnerships. Rather than exploiting pre-existing knowledge to create the future, effectuation logic takes contingencies as given constraints and empowers entrepreneurs to leverage those contingencies. As said earlier, the entrepreneurial notion needs to embrace the control logic rather than a prediction of the future. Therefore, affordable loss, acceptable risk, strategic partnerships, and control logic become four principles based on effectuation theory (Sarasvathy 2001).

In linking effectuation logic with entrepreneurial exploration and exploitation, entrepreneurs may think that decisions related to exploration activities must follow effectuation logic. In contrast, decisions related to exploitation-related activities must follow causation models. Thus, in balancing entrepreneurial exploration and exploitation, both effectuation and causation thinking can be utilized. Rather than looking at these dichotomies as either/or, entrepreneurs must embrace 'both' approaches, and learn to balance these, as and when the environment and the issues at hand demand. While ambidexterity at the entrepreneurial level would be good, genetics have not contributed to shaping such outcomes in large numbers. Only a small percentage of the population are that breed of ambidextrous entrepreneur. However, the models and data science available to entrepreneurs through the adoption of i4.0 may support entrepreneurs' weaknesses to realize the ambidexterity at the entrepreneurial level. Though implications will be discussed in a separate chapter at the end, it is essential to highlight the critical implications of i4.0 research and implementation, together with the impact on globalization, economic nationalism, or populism — the bubble we are witnessing in recent times as triggered by BREXIT and Trumponomics.

**AARRR Model: Acquisition, Activation, Retention, Referral, Revenue.** Though the elaborated discussion will be covered in Chapter 5, it is good to mention that McClure (2007) introduced start-up metrics as AARRR. This concept helped start-ups with the right metrics rather than the old accounting metrics. Our recommendation went to entrepreneurs without judgment, so they could benefit from this metric in the early phase of learning loops and validated learning derived from the hypotheses testing.

## CONCLUSION

As outlined above, the frontier of research is emerging in balancing exploration and exploitation in the age of i4.0. At the summary level, scratching of the innovation potential by testing the assumptions on i4.0BMC has been suggested in this chapter. Still, the new research and practice in integrating design thinking in this area are essential as well. I will touch on this at a superficial level in the customer creation and company development phase. The next book could be written in this chapter and could integrate design thinking into this emerging phenomenon.

Research in finalizing i4.0 BMC is still in infancy as the real-time data access and decision-making models will make the testing of assumptions and growth hypothesis easier and more comfortable. For that matter, linking this concept with the vibrant capitalist culture of the 18$^{th}$ century, as suggested by Phelps (2013), would be a plausible approach. Have we finally democratized the entrepreneurial ecosystem? Are proprietary and closed-door policies a thing of the past? How and when will singularity take place? Such questions may be interesting for the reader's quest for writing in this field.

I look forward to co-authoring these issues to some extent in the future.

All theories and models discussed in the book are mostly conceptual. However, jobs-to-be-done seems credible in an empirical sense as it has already been developed into a book called *Competing with Luck*. However, further empirical research in testing the framework created in this book is highly recommended. As it is comprehensive, and, in many senses replacing the 'soul' of a lean start-up with jobs-to-be-done theory, the future research frontier will be exciting to observe.

It is too early in the emergence of new ways of testing MVDP, value proposition, and growth hypotheses to conclude anything. The phenomenon is recent, and the choice is ours on how we can capitalize on it. However, testing all SVP (sticky, viral, and paid) growth strategies in the digital or serviced world is a must. Gaining a wider understanding of customers' use cases, and testing multiples of those in MVDP, derives the validated learning of which use cases will dominate the customers' buying behavior. This jobs-to-be-done theory approach to cracking the entrepreneurial exploration and exploitation code makes me believe that it will be an excellent service for the entrepreneurial community and academics to have a volume which combines the existing literature. Now the pieces are tied together, from entrepreneurial exploration and exploitation, lean start-ups, and jobs-to-be-done theory. Also, these theories will be complemented by effectuation theory in the decision-making model in Chapter 6.

## REFERENCES

Araya, D. (2013). Thinking forward: Vivek Wadhwa on singularity university. *E-Learning and Digital Media*, *10*(3), 320-323.

Barney, J. (1991). Firm resources and sustained competitive advantage. *Journal of Management*, *17*(1), 99-120.

Baur, C., and Wee, D. (2015). Manufacturing's next act. *McKinsey Quarterly, Jun.*

Bhandari, K. (2017). *Internationalization and Organizational Ambidexterity for Sustainable Performance: Moderating Effects of Firm-specific Advantages and Competitive Strategies*, Acta Wasaensia 379, Vaasan yliopisto, University of Vaasa.

Blank, S. (2013). *The four steps to the epiphany: successful strategies for products that win*. BookBaby.

Bughin, J., Chui, M., and Manyika, J. (2015). An executive's guide to the Internet of Things. *McKinsey Quarterly*.

Burmeister, C., Lüttgens, D., and Piller, F. T. (2016). Business model innovation for Industrie 4.0: why the "Industrial Internet" mandates a new perspective on innovation. *Die Unternehmung*, *70*(2), 124-152.

Chesbrough, H. (2012). Open innovation: Where we've been and where we're going. *Research-Technology Management*, *55*(4), 20-27.

Chang, S., Kogut, B., and Yang, J. S. (2016). Global diversification discount and its discontents: A bit of self-selection makes a world of difference. *Strategic Management Journal*, *37*(11), 2254-2274.

Chesbrough, H. (2006). Open innovation: a new paradigm for understanding industrial innovation. Open innovation: Researching a new paradigm, 400, 0-19.

Eisenmann, T. R. (2008). Managing proprietary and shared platforms. *California Management Review*, *50*(4), 31-53.

Christensen, C. M., Cook, S., and Hall, T. (2005). Marketing malpractice. *Harvard business review*, *83*(12), 74-83.

Christensen, C. M., Hall, T., Dillon, K., and Duncan, D. S. (2016). Know your customers' jobs to be done. *Harvard Business Review*, *94*(9), 54-62.

Denis, D. J., Denis, D. K., and Yost, K. (2002). Global diversification, industrial diversification, and firm value. *The Journal of Finance*, *57*(5), 1951-1979.

Gabrielsson, M., Seppälä, T., and Gabrielsson, P. (2016). Realizing a hybrid competitive strategy and achieving superior financial performance while internationalizing in the high-technology market. *Industrial Marketing Management*, *54*, 141-153.

Frolov, V. G., Kaminchenko, D. I., Kovylkin, D. Y., Alex, J., and Alex, A. (2017). The main economic factors of sustainable manufacturing within the industrial policy concept of industry 4.0. Academy of Strategic Management Journal.

Hall, T., Christensen, C., Dillon, K., and Duncan, D. (2016). Competing Against Luck: The Story of Innovation and Customer Choice. *EUA: HarperBusiness*.

Hart, O., and Zingales, L. (2017). Companies Should Maximize Shareholder Welfare Not Market Value.

Kim, G., and Huh, M. G. (2015). Exploration and organizational longevity: The moderating role of strategy and environment. *Asia Pacific Journal of Management*, *32*(2), 389-414.

Lasi, H., Fettke, P., Kemper, H. G., Feld, T., and Hoffmann, M. (2014). Industry 4.0. *Business and Information Systems Engineering*, *6*(4), 239-242.

Levinthal, D. A., and March, J. G. (1993). The myopia of learning. Strategic management journal, 14(S2), 95-112.

Liao, Y., Deschamps, F., Loures, E. D. F. R., and Ramos, L. F. P. (2017). Past, present, and future of Industry 4.0-a a systematic literature review and research agenda proposal. *International Journal of Production Research*, *55*(12), 3609-3629.

March, J. G. (1991). Exploration and exploitation in organizational learning. *Organization Science*, *2*(1), 71-87.

Marr, B. (June 20, 2016). What Everyone Must Know About Industry 4.0. *Forbes Magazine.* Accessed on 31.07.2017 from https://www.forbes.com/sites/bernardmarr/2016/06/20/what-everyone-must-know-about-industry-4-0/#5ed8a614795f

Mazzei, M. J., and Noble, D. (2017). Big data dreams: A framework for corporate strategy. *Business Horizons*, *60*(3), 405-414.

Moogk, D. R. (2012). Minimum viable product and the importance of experimentation in technology startups. *Technology Innovation Management Review*, *2*(3).

Nambisan, S., Siegel, D., and Kenney, M. (2018). On open innovation, platforms, and entrepreneurship. *Strategic Entrepreneurship Journal*, *12*(3), 354-368.

Porter, M. E., and Kramer, M. R. (2019). Creating shared value. In *Managing sustainable business* (pp. 323-346). Springer, Dordrecht.

Ocasio, W. (1997). Towards an attention-based view of the firm. *Strategic management journal*, 187-206.

Penrose, E. T. (1959). The theory of the growth of the firm. *New York: Sharpe*.

Piketty, T. (2020). *Capital and Ideology*. Cambridge: Harvard University Press.

Porter, M. E., and Advantage, C. (1985). Creating and Sustaining Superior Performancc.

Porter, M. E., and Heppelmann, J. E. (2015). How smart, connected products are transforming companies. *Harvard Business Review*, *93*(10), 96-114.

Ries, E. (2011). *The lean startup: How today's entrepreneurs use continuous innovation to create radically successful businesses*. Crown Books.

Spanos, Y. E., Zaralis, G., and Lioukas, S. (2004). Strategy and industry effects on profitability: evidence from Greece. *Strategic management journal*, *25*(2), 139-165.

Schaefer, D., Walker, J., and Flynn, J. (2017, August). A Data-Driven Business Model Framework for Value Capture in Industry 4.0. In Advances in Manufacturing Technology XXXI: Proceedings of the 15th International Conference on Manufacturing Research, Incorporating the 32nd National Conference on Manufacturing Research, September 5–7, 2017, University of Greenwich, UK (Vol. 6, p. 245). IOS Press.

Strange, R., Strange, R., Zucchella, A., and Zucchella, A. (2017). Industry 4.0, global value chains, and international business. *Multinational Business Review*, *25*(3), 174-184.

Teece, D. J., Pisano, G., and Shuen, A. (1997). Dynamic capabilities and strategic management. *Strategic management journal*, 509-533.

Teece, D. J. (2007). Explicating dynamic capabilities: the nature and microfoundations of (sustainable) enterprise performance. *Strategic management journal*, *28*(13), 1319-1350.

Teece, D. J. (2014). A dynamic capabilities-based entrepreneurial theory of the multinational enterprise. *Journal of International Business Studies*, *45*(1), 8-37.

Uotila, J., Maula, M., Keil, T., and Zahra, S. A. (2009). Exploration, exploitation, and financial performance: analysis of SandP 500 corporations. *Strategic Management Journal*, *30*(2), 221-231.

Vuori, T. O., and Huy, Q. N. (2016). Distributed attention and shared emotions in the innovation process: How Nokia lost the smartphone battle. Administrative Science Quarterly, 61(1), 9-51.

Wade, M., and Hulland, J. (2004). The resource-based view and information systems research: Review, extension, and suggestions for future research. *MIS Quarterly*, *28*(1), 107-142.

## KEY TERMS AND DEFINITIONS

**SVP:** Sticky, viral, and paid growth strategies used in testing the hypothesis in the customer validation phase.

**Sticky growth:** Customers get addicted to the service, and the growth starts through word of mouth.

**Viral growth**: The product itself has a viral component either through the inherent nature of product use or referral process to friends and inner circles. For example, it is evident that to make Facebook successful; one needs to find a way to invite friends to the service.

**Paid growth:** In paid growth, customers or advertisers must get a referral or new customers.

**BM*O*L loop:** Build-measure-optimize-learn loop where progress is validated learning for next iteration or future product decision.

**MV*D*P:** Minimum viable but desirable product at the same time. This is the new, improved conceptualization of the original minimum viable product (MVP), which gave a connotation that quality is compromised in testing the quick and dirty version of the product or service. However, as suggested by Kano's model, "must-be" qualities cannot be compromised even in MVP, for which scholars suggested a new concept of 'desirable' by the customers.

**i4.0BMC:** Industry 4.0 Business Model Canvas. This is the new, improved conceptualization of the original Business Model Canvas (BMC), which was useful but not comprehensive in capturing the details of i4.0 changes. From the older version's nine blocks, the improved version has 11 blocks now. Creating unfair advantage becomes one of the primary vital concepts inside the i4.0BMC.

# CHAPTER 5

# ENTREPRENEURIAL EXPLORATION AND EXPLOITATION: BUSINESS MODEL SEARCH PHASE II


**ABSTRACT**

*As i4.0 takes off, entrepreneurial exploration and exploitation in the business model search phases can be divided into customer discovery and customer validation phases. Chapter 4 touched upon the customer discovery phase, while this chapter focuses on the customer validation phase, where the search is geared towards establishing product-market fit through i4.0BMC discussed in Chapter 3; the focus on finding out the causal link between the product and service with the jobs-to-be-done by the customer must not be left out. The previous chapter's focus was to link open innovation and platformization, in the presence of contingency variables on the potential future performance of the firm, estimated as customer lifetime value (CLV). However, the real measure of progress in this phase is validated learning through the multiple iterations of open innovation activities and platformization efforts. Open digital platforms and platform forking were discussed at length in Chapter 1, but the same could be done to hack the business model in this phase. In this phase, as in the earlier phase, all the interviews were done in blocks of i4.0BMC and tested in a minimum viable, but desirable, product (MVDP) or minimum viable concept (MVC), to understand the more significant product or solution we are going to develop. Such MVDP or MVC reduces the costs of development and failure as an entrepreneur can iterate on the product or service early enough without burning millions of dollars in the illusion of entrepreneurial vision. MVDP allows entrepreneurs to come to the reality and adjust their vision. Once the learning in this phrase suggests that the product is feasible, only then does full prototype or pilot testing of the product start.*



Keywords: Customer discovery, Customer validation, Entrepreneurial exploration, Entrepreneurial exploitation, MVP, i4.0BMC

## INTRODUCTION

The implications of i4.0 are tremendous for companies like Alibaba.com from China, and 'sharing economies', such as Uber and Airbnb. All of these new enterprises are transforming traditional business models and enabling entrepreneurship at the mass level. Balancing exploration and exploitation (March 1991) and its implications for the emerging landscape becomes even more critical. Exploration means searching for new business models and experimenting with the future. But exploration alone will not make for success; one needs to exploit or capture the value in the emerging phenomenon. One of the processes used in navigating such a changing landscape is called the customer development model (Blank 2013). The customer development model has four steps: customer discovery, customer validation, customer creation, and company building (or scaling up). However, the balance of exploration and exploitation depends on how fast a build-measure-optimize-learn (BM*O*L) loop is executed to pursue customer development.

Based on Ries (2011) the BML loop is the development cycle to experiment and learn. But in this chapter, the BM*O*L loop, with the extra *O* representing optimization, is used. The unit of progress is validated learning. Managing under uncertainty needs dynamic capabilities (Teece et al. 1997, Teece 2007) where sensing, seizing, and reconfiguring activities are essential for sustainable performance. Marr (2016) illustrated the way the technological waves shaped our lives in human history. The steam engine and the first machines improved productivity, while electricity enabled assembly line and mass production. The third wave came from the computers that enabled automation. Now is the i4.0 wave, with robotics connected remotely to computer systems and machine learning algorithms, which can learn and control the robotics to realize a 'smart factory'.

Burmeister, Lüttgens, and Piller (2016) not only outlined the emerging new business models supported by i4.0 and platform-based business model; the authors argued that business model innovation is taking place which is changing the firm and industry boundaries alike. Creating a business model is easy, but implementation and support for the same is a daunting task. It is a new paradigm, and it is changing everything we know as a business so far. We need new best practices to surf in this sea of change, build new organizational structures to align the difference with the new reality, and build necessary tools to analyse, optimize, and understand the technology layer, plus its impact on the firm's business model. Existing tools and structures are not ready to grasp the change we are discussing. There were no smart products with the intelligence to transmit data to the cloud servers for analysis through data mining or machine learning and AI, nor were there data scientists in the organizations.

These roles will make the cross-functional, organization-wide change as they have an interface with all the functions to optimize both product and process. Customer service data is real-time, and decision-makers can make immediate corrections if something is not right. At the same time, pursuing entrepreneurial exploration for new ideas that can satisfy customer needs and exploit existing services and products to make a maximum possible profit is possible. Management literature has multiple contributions on how to balance short-term profit and long-term success. However, suppose the CEO is i4.0 competent, for the first time in the history of management. In that case, these two conflicting trade-offs could be reconciled, and innovation and efficiency can go side-by-side.

## BACKGROUND

Over forty years of empirical research has failed to resolve a fundamental question in strategic management literature; how to operate in extreme conditions of uncertainty. A solution-oriented approach would be to ask how a firm can leverage the customer development model for the innovation triggered by i4.0. As is evident from the start-up-related literature, the customer development model (Blank 2013) suggests that under the conditions of uncertainty created by i4.0 technologies, the search for a new business model is crucial. The search starts with customer discovery and customer validation. Here, the goal is to experiment with the customer to test the value proposition so that getting quick feedback and doing iteration is possible. Once the customer need is validated, then scalability is needed. Here, the goal is to create the customer first and build the company at large. In the search phase, validated learning is the only unit of progress to measure in accounting terms. Each customer development model could be iterated by the build-measure-optimize-learn (BM*O*L) loop suggested by Ries (2011) in his book *Lean Start-up.* The higher the uncertainty, the faster the loop, should be the focus. As mentioned earlier, the unit of progress is validated learning. Most theorists believe strategic purity — the extent to which a business pursues one type of generic strategy over another — contributes to better performance. However, the latest findings (Krishna 2017) suggest that pursuing both cost and differentiation strategy, called a hybrid strategy, is feasible.

It took forty years to understand the hybrid strategies in strategic management literature. Over 50 years of research in international business literature has failed to resolve a fundamental internationalization question: how to scale up a venture in the condition of uncertainty. The extant literature has been inconclusive for fifty years. Based on the latest literature, rather than using multiple theories, it is good to focus on the dynamic capabilities-based view (DCV) (Teece et al. 1997, Teece 2007, 2014) to streamline the theoretical contribution. However, dynamic capabilities are dynamic by nature, and tracing them in innovation and scaling activities is extremely challenging. Another implication is that the earlier realization was that the resource-based view (RBV) (1991) and DCV are siblings. However, a recent conclusion after immersion into the theoretical framework and operationalization, is that the resource position barrier, as advocated by the RBV, needs to be leveraged to realize, seize, and orchestrate the DCV. Entrepreneurial management and empowering innovations are only possible from the DCV perspective. The scaling of innovation under extreme uncertainty created by i4.0 moves from advantage-seeking mode to opportunity-seeking mode. Explaining the firm-specific advantages would be more comfortable from the DCV perspective as well. Thus, DCV is a clear theoretical rationale for navigating the business model generated by i4.0 and the discussions in this chapter.

The changes suggested by Burmeister et al. (2016) have some exciting implications for management theory and practice. The new wave offers the possibility for customization of products and services and efficiency optimization at the same time. This will give an edge for those who understand the meaning of adaptation to the individual customer needs. Porter's idea of competitive supremacy based on either cost leadership or differentiation is no longer valid. The new change wave will delete the concept of 'stuck-in-the-middle' syndrome while pursuing both cost leadership and differentiation. The old idea of 'red ocean'-based cut-throat competition is no longer valid. The new 'blue ocean' thinking, where competition becomes irrelevant is becoming a new reality every day. As business level thinking is changing, so does functional level thinking - balancing the trade-off between novelty-centricity and efficiency-centricity (Zott and Amit 2007) in business model design is becoming a reality, illustrated by multiple cases by Burmeister et al. (2016). Thus, both entrepreneurial exploration and exploitation are possible at the same time.

## OPEN INNOVATION AND PLATFORMIZATION

### Issues, Controversies, Problems

Some of the issues are carried over from Chapter 4, a new section of the business model search phase, where customer discovery was detailed as Phase I. In this phase, we take customer validation as Phase II. Therefore, underlying theories and assumptions from Chapter 4 seem similar at this stage also.

**Balancing exploration and exploitation in the age of i4.0.** Following the collapse of Nokia has been interesting, even after leaving the company. Vuori and Huy (2016) found that distributed attention and shared emotions were critical in losing the smartphone battle. In this qualitative study from 2005-2010, when one of the world's best brands collapsed into rubble, they found that top and middle managers' shared emotions in the smartphone innovation process triggered many behaviours that resulted in the demise of the giant. However, one important part of this equation is organizational attention triggering fear among managers. Top managers were scared of external competitors and shareholders, but middle managers were afraid of internal groups, including superiors and peers. There was communication bias, and interpretation bias, between top managers and middle managers. Therefore, attention towards balancing exploration and exploitation was clouded by shared emotions and distributed attention.

Thus, this chapter has implications for theory and practice. The chapter counters the resource fungibility (Penrose 1959) based on the RBT resource immobility logic (Barney 1991) to create a sustainable competitive advantage. Rather than assuming a linear impact on performance, our premise is to seek the optimum level of valuable derived information from the big data that becomes the cornerstone of strategic decision-making. Digitalization improves functional capabilities, shapes industrial innovation, and enables learning breakthroughs (Mazzei and Noble 2017), leading to performance improvement. However, too much or too little, digitalization is not beneficial. There is a need to tune in to the optimum level of digitalization.

**Entrepreneurial exploration.** At the heart of this change is the possibility of simultaneous pursuits of opportunity discovery and creation, divided by academicians for over three decades. While building open innovation models with customers and partners, the exploration crosses the firm and industry boundaries. Who knew a social network like Facebook could get into the money business (through Libra)? Similarly, value creation is happening at a high rate of supported competence in i4.0 technologies in the firm, from the top to the factory floor.

**Entrepreneurial exploitation**. Over the years, the nurturing of the ICT benefitted efficiency projects; however, it will be different this time. While leveraging optimization algorithms in manufacturing and resource allocation, huge benefits come from the new ideas and processes that may become the cornerstone of competitive advantage, or, for that matter, sustainable advantages where all stakeholders benefit from each other. To succeed, a new culture of experimentation, celebrating failure for learning, and meritocracy based on i4.0 skills, must be the focus of the culture as 'culture eats strategy for breakfast'.

## SOLUTIONS AND RECOMMENDATIONS

Though this was discussed in Chapter 4, we reiterate the theories and concepts behind the theoretical model so that readers with access to this chapter can also understand what the guiding theory and entrepreneurial philosophy are.

**Jobs-to-be-done Theory**. As discussed in the context of the larger framework, the BMOL loop finally gets its guiding theory to solve the jobs-to-be-done by the customers or various use cases and storyboards related to scenario testing. In this core process, earlier notions collected more correlational attributes, but now, with Christensen et al.'s (2016) approach, a causal link between the product or service and customers' buying behaviour is identified. This tool gives a strong foundation that becomes finally feasible, as suggested in *Competing Against Luck* (Hall, Christensen, Dillon, and Duncan, 2016). According to the authors, it is more a matter of understanding customer choices and their behaviour in making purchase decisions. This removes correlation in the process and builds causality in the real sense. Using a guiding theory like jobs-to-be-done makes the next phase of the entrepreneurial wave far more exciting, while embedding this into the lean start-up concepts. However, with the theory's umbrella concept, the whole lean testing and development gets a new meaning and hypotheses — building causality in the system from the correlational attributes of customer's buying behaviour.

**Customer Development Model**. Most of the start-up entrepreneurial ecosystem targeting industry 4.0 is recommended to follow customer development (Blank 2013) together with i4.0BMC. The four steps to epiphany are the four steps in the customer development model: discovery, validation, creation, and scale. During the customer discovery phase, the key hypotheses should test the customer/problem fit. Similarly, during the customer validation phase, the key hypotheses should test the problem/solution fit. During the customer creation phase, the key hypotheses should test the solution/customer fit. Finally, during the scaling phase solution/channel fit, related hypotheses are tested. This hypothesis-driven development is the secret recipe of significant innovations coming from entrepreneurial ecosystems, or Silicon Valley, as a starting point.

Artificial intelligence (AI), the Internet of Things (IoT), cloud computing, big data, and automation, summarized together as digitalization or, for that matter, the need for exploration and related changes in the business model, has triggered a new industrial wave called Industry 4.0 (i4.0). To understand such a phenomenon, the existing conceptualization of exploration, as suggested by March (1991), is valid. I extended March's (1991) definition of exploration and exploitation, where exploration is described by exploring, searching, and experimenting, while exploitation is described by activities such as exploitation, refinement, efficiency, etc.

**Build-Measure-Optimize-Learn (BMOL) Loop**. The build-measure-optimize-learn (BMOL) loop, as discussed in Chapter 3, is the execution loop in hypothesis-driven development, and the essence of searching for a business model and later, the execution of a business model. Lean start-up thinking discussed only the BML loop, but to be successful in i4.0, the loop must have an 'optimize' stage. As discussed earlier, under the high level of uncertainty created by i4.0, it is essential to understand that this loop needs to be faster. However, new thinking in the BMOL loop, that the algorithm-based systems optimizing loops are more critical, and the model can predict the future, needs to be considered. Thus, predictive analytics becomes a holy grail of innovation management (searching for a business model and scaling the company).

**Building Customer Intimacy**

Blank (2013) suggested that the start-ups must listen to the customers to test their vision through a plethora of hypotheses guided by the i4.0BMC. During the customer discovery and validation phase, the only job is to search for a business model. The test of the critical hypotheses from the i4.0BMC to figure out the value proposition to unfair advantages must be tested and pivoted. If they are wrong, once the customer validation is proven, only then can building a company and scaling up begin. During the iteration, it is most likely that the start-up will fail many times. It is crucial to listen to customers early enough, so that even if you fail, you fail fast and learn from it, with little resources.

Blank's (2013) conceptualization of the customer development model has primarily two components: the business model search, and the execution section. The first section embodies customer discovery and customer validation. The second section embodies customer creation and company building, or scaling the startup, as shown in Figure 1.

1. During the customer discovery phase, assumptions or hypotheses are tested to determine problem-solution fit through proposed MVP and proposed funnel (s).
2. During the customer validation phase, the product market, business model validation, and sales and marketing roadmap.
3. During the pivot, unless and until the business model is valid and there is product-market fit, you do not settle, but keep on iterating the test with the discovery and validation cycle to search for a business model.
4. During the customer creation phase, the sole purpose is to scale the execution. Perhaps this is where the companies fail due to wrong timing or premature scaling.
5. The last phase is the company building phase, where scale organization, and scale operations are executed. The later parts, 4 and 5, are called business model execution.

In much of my mentoring to entrepreneurs, I have used the bubble chart in assessing the opportunity at the customer discovery phase, as shown in Figure 2, supported by Figure 3. Figure 3 illustrates the level of likelihood of occurrence of the opportunity apart from its potential. Multiplying both gives the opportunity level, which can be plotted on the bubble chart, where the larger the bubble, the better the opportunity, and vice-versa.

Emerging start-up literature questions the old paradigm of developing fully-fledged products based on the entrepreneur's vision and raises some concerns, as we are dealing with unknowns in the future. The entrepreneur needs to understand the product's value or service and the growth hypothesis to be tested. However, in i4.0BMC, one needs to make sure that optimization loops run faster or, if possible, on a real-time basis. This makes the decision cycles faster, and testing of all value hypothesis and growth hypothesis becomes a fruitful exercise. Under the hypothesis for growth, SVP (Sticky, Viral, and Paid) decisions are crucial, and all three must be tested. In such testing, founders must use the right measures or metrics. Accounting-based metrics do not serve the purpose of understanding the value and growth hypothesis. For example, AARRR (Attention, Acquisition, Retention, Revenue, and Referral) cohort metrics would be a plausible approach, elaborated in the solutions section later. Ries (2011) even called for the removal of old accounting metrics and named it ‘vanity metrics’. However, we are not against accounting measures, but we instead introduce CLV into the dependent or outcome variable rather than ROA or ROS or profit as a metric.

Though discussed in detail in Chapter 4, it is very important to revisit the i4.0BMC. Based on Schaefer, Walker, and Flynn (2017), data-driven business models will be the new norm, rather than an exception. Such business models have created new market segments, economies of scale, and barriers to entry. Indeed, there are weaknesses and threats for which alertness is recommended while creating SO strategies for the future where new i4.0 BMC is optimized through real-time algorithm-based AI and cloud-computing solutions where platformization open innovation is the norm, rather than the exception.

This is the guiding tool in understanding the jobs-to-be-done by the customers. Earlier notions aimed for correlational attributes, with the concept of jobs-to-be-done as a theoretical lens; we assert that we need to build a causal understanding of customers’ buying decisions. In making that approach, founders must not forget the assumptions testing to create an unfair advantage.

The 11 elements of i4.0BMC are listed below, and a brief discussion about each element is presented from the eye of the business model SEARCH angle. However, the underlying theory is to match the jobs-to-be-done with the product attributes and solutions to compete against luck in entrepreneurial pursuits, where causality rules, not the correlation of attributes. Though it’s a repetition from an earlier chapter, we need to make sure that readers can fully understand each chapter in the absence of the others.

1. Key partners
2. Key activities
3. Key resources (metrics)
4. Value proposition
5. Unfair advantages
6. Customer segments

7. Channels
8. Cost structure
9. Revenue structure
10. Social and environmental costs
11. Social and environmental benefit

**Cost Structure and Revenue Streams**. Although the cost structure will be performance-driven, upfront investments are needed to trigger the transformation project. The right side of such a transformation, innovation, or venture, is that subscription business models are feasible, as founders could charge a usage-based fee, and after-sales service could be a revenue stream. In earlier transformations, IT only enabled cost efficiency, but in this new transformation, i4.0 enables new revenue and business model streams, which is the reason the world's best companies are fighting over a pie made out of such transformative technology and emerging business models.

**Social and Environmental Cost and Benefit**. In traditional business models, entrepreneurs needed to think for differentiation advantage or cost leadership so that the venture can achieve sustainable competitive advantage. However, in the i4.0 era, the business model itself is built around the unfair advantages created by i4.0. Provided the entrepreneur finds the business model anchored in these unfair advantages, the business is sustainable in the long run, and competition becomes irrelevant.

Everyone is trying to create their 'blue ocean' where there is no cut-throat competition as in the 'red ocean'. Creating a small street and becoming a monopolist in that street is far better than competing on a highway of multiple competitors for the same business model where profit is the main motive. This novelty makes the i4.0 BMC a unique contribution to synthesis from various authors' contributions, as listed in Figure 4.

However, tools and technologies are neither good nor bad in themselves. How the user of the technology uses that technology rests on hem/her. In this perspective, the morality of users of capitalism to keep competition alive as free and fair competition drives innovation, and progress must be safeguarded. Otherwise, the world will lose the thin hope of creative destruction suggested by Schumpeter, and the fundamental tenets of capitalism to correct itself becomes unfeasible.

As briefly outlined in the issues and controversies, using effectuation theory in making MVP decisions and pivot or persevere decisions after customer validation - the logic of control - can be used. As far as you can control the future outcome, you do not need to predict it. You co-create the future in harmony with the environment, with the logic of how much you can afford to lose, rather than the expected return. Rather than focusing on the competitive advantages, the entrepreneur may build competitive models of strategic alliances and partnerships. Rather than exploiting pre-existing knowledge to create the future, effectuation logic takes contingencies as given constraints, and empowers entrepreneurs to leverage those contingencies. Thus, as said earlier, the entrepreneurial notion needs to embrace the control logic rather than a prediction of the future. Therefore, affordable loss, acceptable risk, strategic partnerships, and control logic, become four principles based on effectuation theory (Sarasvathy 2001).

In linking the effectuation logic with entrepreneurial exploration and exploitation, entrepreneurs may think that the decisions related to exploration activities must follow effectuation logic. In contrast, decisions related to exploitation-related activities must follow causation models. Thus, in balancing entrepreneurial exploration and exploitation, the entrepreneur can utilize both effectuation and causation thinking. Rather than looking at these dichotomies as either/or, entrepreneurs must embrace both approaches and learn to balance them, as and when the environment and the issues at hand demand. While ambidexterity at the entrepreneurial level would be good, genetics have not contributed to shaping such outcomes in large numbers. Only a small percentage of the population are that breed of ambidextrous entrepreneurs. However, the models and data science available to entrepreneurs through the adoption of i4.0 may mitigate an entrepreneur's weaknesses to realize the entrepreneurial level's ambidexterity.

Though implications will be covered in a separate chapter at the end, it is important to highlight the critical implications of i4.0 research and implementation together with the impact on globalization, economic nationalism, or populism; the bubble we are witnessing in recent times, as triggered by BREXIT and Trumponomics.

## Growth Hacking

Conway and Hemphill's (2019) growth model search and execution is an exciting approach. This model is right when the customer discovery and validation phase in the business model search-phase is ongoing. Revisiting the same model in the following Chapters 6 and 7 in the growth phase would be interesting in linking the portfolio approach of decision making for growth. The model is based on an approach of generating growth in a sample from UK technology sectors. The keyword used in the paper is 'growth-hacking,' which, as per the authors, is a 'data-informed' marketing approach. Not only that, the focus on digital marketing makes the approach even popular and more comfortable to adapt. However, the model is similar in the frame to lean start-up thinking, with 'proof-of-concept' in place of MVP used in lean thinking. Figure 3 shows two distinct phases: the search phase and the execution phase. In this section, the discussion on the search phase makes sense, as we are in the validation phase of the i4.0BMC.

Yes, it is more or less data science-based growth hacking, but it also scans the environment to discover, create, and recognize emerging opportunities before the competitor does. Acquiring people with the sense of the future and deriving meaning from the data is a daunting task. Also, there is a need not to abandon traditional marketing to fill the vacuum between the physical and digital world. It is a mindset and process to utilize limited resources to scale up the technology start-ups. Some literature also talks about agile marketing for the same or similar concepts. Once the business model is found and validated, it is then the marketing and sales task to replicate it in multiple deals. Building customer loyalty and retention, a referral framework, and, if possible, a push for virality is the first choice, but other techniques in SVP should not be ruled out. Sticky, or paid, growth is also viable.

**AARRR Model: Acquisition, Activation, Retention, Referral, Revenue.** McClure (2007) introduced AARRR as start-up metrics. During the marketing and sales process, customer acquisition becomes the challenge of an organization. However, only a few customers activate, visit the website, and sign up in the system or service the start-up is offering. Not all of the signed customers will be retained. A start-up's challenge is to ensure that the benefit exceeds its customers' expectations at every touchpoint. Once a current customer is retained, a fraction of them like the service, refer it to others, and make it accessible to all through social media channels. This endorsement causes the company to gain new growth. However, referral alone does not solve the income equation. Some of these referred customers need to buy the product or service to generate revenue.

In summary:

**Acquisition:** Users come to the site from various channels.

**Activation:** User enjoys the first visit, resulting in a 'happy' user experience.

**Retention:** Users come back, and visit the site multiple times.

**Referral:** Users like the product enough to refer others.

**Revenue:** Users conduct some monetization behaviour.

## FUTURE RESEARCH DIRECTIONS

As outlined above, the frontier of research is emerging in balancing exploration and exploitation in the age of i4.0. At summary level, the scratching of the innovation potential by testing the assumptions on the i4.0BMC has been suggested in this chapter, but new research and practice in integrating the design thinking in this area are essential. I will touch on this in the customer creation and company development phase at a superficial level, but the next book could be written on this chapter only, and combining design thinking into this emerging phenomenon.

Research in finalizing i4.0 BMC is still in infancy, as the real-time data access and decision-making models will make the testing of assumptions and growth hypothesis easier and more comfortable. For that matter, linking this concept with the vibrant capitalist culture of the 18$^{th}$ century, as suggested by Phelps (2013), would be a plausible approach. Have we finally democratized the entrepreneurial ecosystem? Is it so? Will the proprietary and closed-door policies be a thing of the past? How and when will singularity take place? Such questions would make the reader's quest for writing in this field interesting.

## CONCLUSION

It is too early to conclude anything in the emergence of new ways of testing MVDP, value proposition, and growth hypotheses. The phenomenon is recent, and the choice is ours on how we can capitalize on it. However, testing all SVP (sticky, viral, and paid) growth strategies in the digital or servitized world is necessary. Gaining a more comprehensive understanding of customers' use cases, and testing multiples of those in MVDP, derives the validated learning of which use cases will be dominant in the buying behaviour of customers. This jobs-to-be-done theory approach to cracking the entrepreneurial exploration and exploitation code made me believe that it will be an excellent service for the entrepreneurial community and academics to have a volume that combines the existing literature. The pieces are tied up together from entrepreneurial exploration and exploitation, to lean start-up, and jobs-to-be-done theory. Also, these theories will be complemented by effectuation theory in the decision-making model in Chapter 6.

## REFERENCES

Burmeister, C., Lüttgens, D., and Piller, F. T. (2016). Business model innovation for Industrie 4.0: why the "Industrial Internet" mandates a new perspective on innovation. *Die Unternehmung*, *70*(2), 124-152.

Chesbrough, H. (2012). Open innovation: Where we've been and where we're going. *Research-Technology Management*, *55*(4), 20-27.

Chesbrough, H. (2006). Open innovation: a new paradigm for understanding industrial innovation. Open innovation: Researching a new paradigm, 400, 0-19.

Eisenmann, T. R. (2008). Managing proprietary and shared platforms. *California Management Review*, *50*(4), 31-53.

Frolov, V. G., Kaminchenko, D. I., Kovylkin, D. Y., Alex, J., and Alex, A. (2017). The main economic factors of sustainable manufacturing within the industrial policy concept of industry 4.0. Academy of Strategic Management Journal.

Moogk, D. R. (2012). Minimum viable product and the importance of experimentation in technology startups. *Technology Innovation Management Review*, *2*(3).

Nambisan, S., Siegel, D., and Kenney, M. (2018). On open innovation, platforms, and entrepreneurship. *Strategic Entrepreneurship Journal*, *12*(3), 354-368.

Porter, M. E., and Kramer, M. R. (2019). Creating shared value. In *Managing sustainable business* (pp. 323-346). Springer, Dordrecht.

Schaefer, D., Walker, J., and Flynn, J. (2017, August). A Data-Driven Business Model Framework for Value Capture in Industry 4.0. In Advances in Manufacturing Technology XXXI: Proceedings of the 15th International Conference on Manufacturing Research, Incorporating the 32nd National Conference on Manufacturing Research, September 5–7, 2017, University of Greenwich, UK (Vol. 6, p. 245). IOS Press.

Barney, J. (1991). Firm resources and sustained competitive advantage. *Journal of Management*, *17*(1), 99-120.

Baur, C., and Wee, D. (2015). Manufacturing's next act. *McKinsey Quarterly, Jun.*

Bhandari, K. (2017). *Internationalization and Organizational Ambidexterity for Sustainable Performance: Moderating Effects of Firm-specific*

*Advantages and Competitive Strategies*, Acta Wasaensia 379, Vaasan yliopisto, University of Vaasa.
Blank, S. (2013). *The four steps to the epiphany: successful strategies for products that win*. BookBaby.
Bughin, J., Chui, M., and Manyika, J. (2015). An executive's guide to the Internet of Things. *McKinsey Quarterly*.
Chang, S., Kogut, B., and Yang, J. S. (2016). Global diversification discount and its discontents: A bit of self-selection makes a world of difference. *Strategic Management Journal*, *37*(11), 2254-2274.
Denis, D. J., Denis, D. K., and Yost, K. (2002). Global diversification, industrial diversification, and firm value. *The Journal of Finance*, *57*(5), 1951-1979.
Gabrielsson, M., Seppälä, T., and Gabrielsson, P. (2016). Realizing a hybrid competitive strategy and achieving superior financial performance while internationalizing in the high-technology market. *Industrial Marketing Management*, *54*, 141-153.
Hart, O., and Zingales, L. (2017). Companies Should Maximize Shareholder Welfare Not Market Value.
Kim, G., and Huh, M. G. (2015). Exploration and organizational longevity: The moderating role of strategy and environment. *Asia Pacific Journal of Management*, *32*(2), 389-414.
Lasi, H., Fettke, P., Kemper, H. G., Feld, T., and Hoffmann, M. (2014). Industry 4.0. *Business and Information Systems Engineering*, *6*(4), 239-242.
Levinthal, D. A., and March, J. G. (1993). The myopia of learning. Strategic management journal, 14(S2), 95-112.
Liao, Y., Deschamps, F., Loures, E. D. F. R., and Ramos, L. F. P. (2017). Past, present, and future of Industry 4.0-a a systematic literature review and research agenda proposal. *International Journal of Production Research*, *55*(12), 3609-3629.
Marr, B. (June 20, 2016). What Everyone Must Know About Industry 4.0. *Forbes Magazine.* Accessed on 31.07.2017 from https://www.forbes.com/sites/bernardmarr/2016/06/20/what-everyone-must-know-about-industry-4-0/#5ed8a614795f
March, J. G. (1991). Exploration and exploitation in organizational learning. *Organization Science*, *2*(1), 71-87.
Mazzei, M. J., and Noble, D. (2017). Big data dreams: A framework for corporate strategy. *Business Horizons*, *60*(3), 405-414.
Ocasio, W. (1997). Towards an attention-based view of the firm. *Strategic management journal*, 187-206.

Penrose, E. T. (1959). The theory of the growth of the firm. *New York: Sharpe.*

Porter, M. E., and Advantage, C. (1985). Creating and Sustaining Superior Performance.

Porter, M. E., and Heppelmann, J. E. (2015). How smart, connected products are transforming companies. *Harvard Business Review*, *93*(10), 96-114.

Ries, E. (2011). *The lean startup: How today's entrepreneurs use continuous innovation to create radically successful businesses*. Crown Books.

Spanos, Y. E., Zaralis, G., and Lioukas, S. (2004). Strategy and industry effects on profitability: evidence from Greece. *Strategic management journal*, *25*(2), 139-165.

Strange, R., Strange, R., Zucchella, A., and Zucchella, A. (2017). Industry 4.0, global value chains, and international business. *Multinational Business Review*, *25*(3), 174-184.

Teece, D. J., Pisano, G., and Shuen, A. (1997). Dynamic capabilities and strategic management. *Strategic management journal*, 509-533.

Teece, D. J. (2007). Explicating dynamic capabilities: the nature and microfoundations of (sustainable) enterprise performance. *Strategic management journal*, *28*(13), 1319-1350.

Teece, D. J. (2014). A dynamic capabilities-based entrepreneurial theory of the multinational enterprise. *Journal of International Business Studies*, *45*(1), 8-37.

Uotila, J., Maula, M., Keil, T., and Zahra, S. A. (2009). Exploration, exploitation, and financial performance: analysis of SandP 500 corporations. *Strategic Management Journal*, *30*(2), 221-231.

Vuori, T. O., and Huy, Q. N. (2016). Distributed attention and shared emotions in the innovation process: How Nokia lost the smartphone battle. Administrative Science Quarterly, 61(1), 9-51.

Wade, M., and Hulland, J. (2004). The resource-based view and information systems research: Review, extension, and suggestions for future research. *MIS Quarterly*, *28*(1), 107-142.

## KEY TERMS AND DEFINITIONS

**SVP:** Sticky, viral, and paid growth strategies used in testing the hypothesis in the customer validation phase.

**Sticky growth:** Customers get addicted to the service, and the growth starts through word of mouth.

**Viral growth**: The product itself has a viral component either through the inherent nature of product use or referral process to friends and inner circles. For example, it is evident that to make Facebook successful; one needs to find a way to invite friends to the service.

**Paid growth:** In paid growth, customers or advertisers must get a referral or new customers.

**BM*O*L loop:** Build-measure-optimize-learn loop where progress is validated learning for next iteration or future product decision.

**MV*D*P:** Minimum viable but desirable product at the same time. This is the new, improved conceptualization of the original minimum viable product (MVP), which gave a connotation that quality is compromised in testing the quick and dirty version of the product or service. However, as suggested by Kano's model, "must-be" qualities cannot be compromised even in MVP, for which scholars suggested a new concept of 'desirable' by the customers.

**i4.0BMC:** Industry 4.0 Business Model Canvas. This is the new, improved conceptualization of the original Business Model Canvas (BMC), which was useful but not comprehensive in capturing the details of i4.0 changes. From the older version's nine blocks, the improved version has 11 blocks now. Creating unfair advantage becomes one of the primary key concepts inside the i4.0BMC.

# CHAPTER 6

# ENTREPRENEURIAL EXPLORATION AND EXPLOITATION: PERSEVERE OR PIVOT DECISION


## ABSTRACT

*Decisions regarding entrepreneurial exploration and exploitation, and the resulting challenge of maintaining the balance thereof, demand critical judgment enabled by validated customer discovery and validation learning. In both of these phases, the goal was to build a causal understanding of the product and features with the customer's jobs-to-be-done while using the product and feature. If the product-market fit has been realized, the entrepreneur must continue on the same path to explore market growth. In this chapter, reasons for startup failure and, for that matter, large corporations' new line of business failure (excluding small and medium-sized enterprises) is discussed.*



Keywords: Entrepreneurial Decision, Iterate, Optimize, Validated learning, Product-market fit, Startups, Large corporations.

## INTRODUCTION

During my entrepreneurial exploration in multinationals and the startup world alike, I encountered that most promising business ideas or startup ideas fail at the scaling up point — meaning when one needs to pivot or persevere (Ries 2011). This resonates with the *Startup Genome* report (Marmer, Herrmann, Dogrultan, Berman, Eesley, and Blank 2011) which found that premature scaling is the primary cause of failure. The underlying question now, is to ask whether new waves of technologies in industry 4.0 will enable more mature scaling up or not. In my view, as the products and services are becoming smart and interconnected, and consumers collaborate in designing products and services, such a decision may become less challenging, and more startups or business projects in startups and large firms will also be productive. The highest number of observations in the pivot or persevere stage indicates that most of the time, firms pass the gate without thinking whether the product-market fit is there or not. If we recall Moore (2002), it may be a false feeling that the customers we have at the customer validation stage will continue to market us throughout the product lifecycle.

In the causation world, planning is essential, driven by the end goal or result, while in the effectuation world (Sarasvathy 2001), the means-driven logic of entrepreneurial opportunity creation occurs where one starts with who I am, whom I know, and what I can do; in other words, counting your blessings and leveraging your contingencies to configure the resources available to come up with a plausible opportunity with stakeholder interaction. In this emergence, decision-making is more experimentation-based and facts from real-life nurture the intuition of an entrepreneur to avoid premature scaling. If we follow causation logic, perhaps even at this stage, facts cannot just be extrapolated, because we are talking about the emerging nature of i4.0 and related business models. In earlier models, if effectuation was there, it was implicit. My notion here is, however, to make it explicit. While conducting entrepreneurial exploration, follow effectuation logic, and while conducting entrepreneurial exploitation, follow the causation logic of decision-making, rather than arguing about which school of thought you belong to. Let us leave that debate to the scholars in the field. The practitioners' critical lesson is to follow what works in reality, as they do not belong or conform to a school of thought.

## PERSEVERE OR PIVOT

### Issues, Controversies, Problems

During my entrepreneurial exploration in the multinational and startup worlds alike, I encountered that most promising business ideas or startup ideas fail at the juncture of persevere or pivot stage — meaning when they need to pivot, companies scale up. This resonates with the *Startup Genome* report (Marmer, Herrmann, Dogrultan, Berman, Eesley, and Blank 2011). The underlying question now, is to ask whether new waves of technologies will enable more mature scaling or not. In my view, as products and services are becoming smart and interconnected, and consumers collaborate in designing products and services, such a decision problem may become less challenging, and more startups or business projects in large firms will also be productive. The highest number of observations in the pivot or persevere stage in Figure 1 indicates that, most of the time, firms pass the gate without thinking whether the product-market fit is there or not. If we recall Moore (2002), it may be a false feeling that the customer we have at the customer validation stage will continue to market us throughout the product lifecycle. According to *Crossing the Chasm* (Moore 2002) it is a grand challenge for businesses in planning to scale up the product or venture.

Around 32% of ventures scale prematurely. Another 18% fail in the customer validation process, and 17% of the firms fail to build the company even if they have done well in the persevere phase. Similarly, 16% of firms fail due to the founders' attention span on vital strategic issues related to products, markets, and product-market fit, as shown in Figure 1. Only 10% of companies fail to create the customer, while only 7% of the firms fail due to not figuring out the real customer in the early phase of idea generation. These percentages reveal a pattern that entrepreneurs are good at entrepreneurial exploration, but bad at entrepreneurial exploitation. Thus, the founders' teams must balance these skills. Usually, finding an ambidextrous entrepreneur is very hard, but building an ambidextrous founding team is possible. From day one, the firm's focus must be on creating innovative products, but at the same time, they need to build a solid revenue pipeline so that the firm succeeds in taking off before it is too late; however, premature scaling is not an option.

The book by Moore (2002) called *Crossing the Chasm* is a classic to understand how startups can cross from the stage of early adoption to mass-market customers. Moore's other work, called *Escape Velocity*, similarly, tries to understand diversification (related or unrelated) by large firms. Thus, the same author looks at the nature of different sizes and stages of firms. However, with the emergence of a new wave of new technology, products, business models, and machine intelligence, those existing models fall short, as suggested by Porter and Heppelman (2014, 2015). In earlier waves, automation and efficiency were the key drivers; in the new wave, collaboration with all partners, including customers, is the need. Thus, the emergence of new cloud infrastructure will provide a massive new market for technology giants and startups alike. Therefore, neither of the books discusses the decision science needed at each stage of failure or success. As outlined briefly in the introduction section, this chapter takes a broader look into the decision science while exploring and exploiting, and how to balance these for optimization of customer lifetime value.

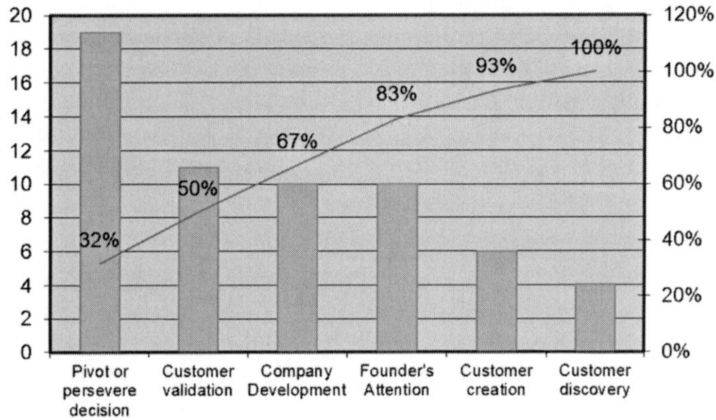


Figure 6-1 Pareto Map for Startup Failure (Based on Author's Observations)

*Crossing the Chasm* (Moore 2002) outlines a grand challenge for businesses planning to scale up the product or venture. Around 32% of ventures scale prematurely. Another 18% fail in the customer validation process, and 17% of the firms fail to build the company even if they have done well in the persevere phase. Similarly, 16% of the firms fail due to the founders' attention span on key strategic issues related to products, markets, and product-market fit, as shown in Figure 1. Only 10% of companies fail to create the customer, while only 7% of the firms fail due to not figuring out the real customer in the early phase of idea generation. These percentages reveal a pattern that entrepreneurs are good at entrepreneurial exploration but bad at entrepreneurial exploitation - innovation comes easily, but revenue does not.

## SOLUTIONS AND RECOMMENDATIONS

### Impact of customer lifetime value

When entrepreneurial exploration or exploitation starts in a venture, balancing these dichotomies is an ardent task, as discussed earlier. This is not because startups do not understand the need for it, but the mere fact that the conflicting goals which these two concepts embody make the activities challenging. Therefore, managing the embeddedness of exploration and exploitation, simultaneously in general, or even in punctuated equilibrium or serially, is challenging. This demands the entrepreneurs' deliberate attention to reorient their organizations whenever they go beyond the limit of either exploration or exploitation. To manage these conflicting activities, startups are increasingly using customer lifetime value (CLV) as their outcome variable, which measures sustainable progress, compared to large company indicators such as profit and ROA. The former approach keeps the customer-first philosophy in their DNA. Simultaneously, the latter focuses on shareholders' value maximization, or profit maximization, at any cost to the environment and society at large. For startups also, there is no excuse for not considering shareholder value maximization as an ultimate goal, or even a better indicator of stakeholder's value maximization, however the path to that audacious goal demands a discipline of execution driven by customer intimacy to deliver product or service differentiation.

The art of balance, as discussed above, needs multilevel thinking at the firm level, team level, and individual level. Having customer-first philosophy at the firm level is mandatory, but the founders, and product and customer teams, must have the mindset and the art (not only science) of carrying out ambidextrous (both exploration and exploitation) activities simultaneously. The majority of workers have difficulties in multi-tasking, and based on my observations in startups, I got involved. But recently, a trend is increasing for training employees to work in all functions during the early phase of the startup, building cross-functional understanding. Thus, job rotation not only inside the function but also in cross-functional teams is highly recommended. The inherent tension between engineering and marketing is dissolved through multi-stack workers in technology startups or product teams and marketing teams in other non-technical product and service startups. However, the latter are becoming part of the past, as industry 4.0 (i4.0) is inherently introducing smartness, automation, cloud computing, and efficiency-driven technologies in any product or company of concern.

The approach taken to build ambidextrous teams may take time, attention, and guidance from the founders in the short-term, but the first validated learning of the mindset would propel the startup to the next level of innovation and agility in the long-term. When such teams are built to empathize with each other's goals and priorities, the tension created by the conflicting goals of short-term profit versus long-term stakeholder's value maximization fades away — and the culture or art of balancing entrepreneurial exploration and exploitation flourishes.

The assumptions of customer-first philosophy come from the logic that if we can satisfy customers' needs and the customer becomes loyal, the customers' lifetime value for the startup is very high. In this notion, customer loyalty and satisfaction are already thoughtfully considered. However, suppose entrepreneurs are only looking for short-term profit. In that case, they may be blinded by the obvious in not focusing on new product development and innovation, undermining the startup's success in the long-term. Thus, balancing entrepreneurial exploration and exploitation to optimize CLV becomes the first lofty goal, ensuring shareholders' value maximization in the second horizon, and finally reaching the stakeholder's value maximization in the third horizon if we observe the three circles in Figure 2.

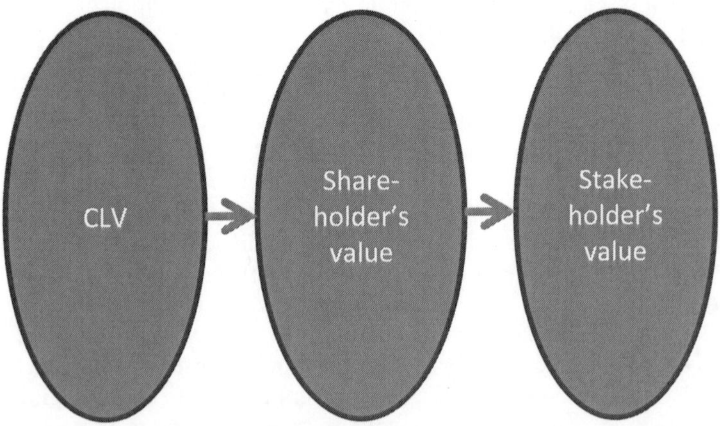


Figure 6-2 Linking customer lifetime value, shareholder's value, and stakeholder's value (Author's conceptualization based on Stahl et al. (2003))

Stahl et al. (2003) argue that CLV is becoming a crucial outcome variable to maintain long-term profitable customer relationships. It is the most valued driver in customer acquisition and retention decisions. However, how the customer-first philosophy brings value to shareholders and stakeholders is still in the research phase. Based on Stahl et al. (2003), there are four CLV components: base potential, growth potential, networking potential, and learning potential. The base potential is estimated through the cashflow generated from the core of the relationship. At the same time, if entrepreneurs can cross-sell and up-brand, it is called growth potential. Similarly, networking potential is generated through the customer's word-of-mouth and referrals, but the cashflow from the knowledge created through the interaction within the relationship becomes the learning potential. The four potentials thus drive the CLV.

Paul, Elango, and Kundu (2019) brought a new dimension by introducing a new construct, 'social responsibility skepticism' (SRS), as an outcome variable of shareholder and stakeholder perspectives. Entrepreneurial ventures may use this angle of keeping an eye on the SRS but without forgetting their major orientations of shareholders' value or, for that matter, stakeholders' value maximization. These two constructs could be considered independent of each other and can be called shareholder-emphasizing perspective (SHEP) and stakeholder-emphasizing perspective (STEP). The findings suggest that the managers accepting either SHEP or STEP have lower SRS. STEP and SHEP can be thought of as two independent constructs to lower SRS, although STEP is better at pursuing that goal. At manager level, the response of STEP is higher. Entrepreneurs or entrepreneurial managers require an understanding of decisions taking social responsibility into consideration. This study demonstrates that grounding in stakeholder and/or shareholder theory can reduce SRS and build a harmonious society. Thus, entrepreneurial exploration and exploitation-based thinking must incorporate STEP as a better choice, but SHEP may help as well. However, with global warming and climate change, and social-plus-income inequality the world faces, STEP must be the guiding mantra in reducing SRS.

CLV is highly important, but the existing accounting systems are not focused on customers, and revenue and costs are not allocated to each customer, but to functions and regions. Even if we allocate costs to each customer account, and follow receivables, estimating non-monetary benefits is not clear. Normally, profit and loss accounts are considered over a year, or even quarterly, but CLV — in name itself — discusses customer relationships' whole life span, which may be longer than 3 or 5 years. Therefore, if an entrepreneur wants to calculate CLV, he needs to build a separate system of accounting other than that used in annual reports, which not only allocates cost and revenue to each customer account, but also captures all four dimensions (base, growth, networking, and learning potentials) through Net Present Value (NPV) of future cash flows, plus an estimation of relationship risks (Stahl et al. 2003).

Kumar et al. (2008) illustrate the International Business Machine (IBM) case, using CLV to indicate customer profitability and allocation of marketing resources. The resource allocation and revenue benefits of IBM's pilot study, conducted for about 35,000 customers using CLV, were in the range of $20 million (a tenfold increase) without any changes in marketing investment level. This differential impact makes us think that startups and large firms optimize their processes and activities with a bad outcome variable so far. Thus, it is not only startups, but large companies that are also gearing towards CLV. However, my argument is that CLV is highly important in entrepreneurial pursuits in startups and large multinationals. In balancing exploration and exploitation in an entrepreneurial venture, the resource allocation, and customer acquisition, and retention are highly susceptible to existing metrics of ROA or other metrics. Ries (2010) called these 'vanity metrics' and suggested that innovation accounting needs to be adopted. Thus, using CLV as an optimization variable for all inputs would be highly important.

The innovator's dilemma is how long one needs to wait for a product to succeed or to change the product features so that there is a product-market fit. However, waiting for too long in one test BMOL loop may be costly. On average, three iterations are needed before finding this product-market fit, but in the i4.0 era, innovation may have real-time optimization, and these iterations may be less. The earlier lean start-up concepts did not follow the pivot or persevere loop in the idea development stage, as shown in Figure 2. However, this book's thesis is that ideas need to be refined through a pivot or persevere logic, through design thinking, where use cases are thought through, and prototypes are built before freezing the concept. This needs to be embedded in detail in the customer discovery phase itself. Such a process would keep product failure to a minimum.

**Jobs-to-be-done Theory.** As discussed in the context of the larger framework, the BMOL loop also gets its guiding theory, finally, to solve the jobs-to-be-done by the customers or various use cases and storyboards related to scenario testing. In this core process, in earlier notions, more correlational attributes were collected, but now, with Christensen et al.'s (2016) approach, a causal link between the product or service and the buying behavior of the customer is identified. This tool gives a strong foundation that finally becomes feasible, as outlined in *Competing Against Luck* (Hall, Christensen, Dillon, and Duncan 2016). According to the authors, it is more about understanding customers' choices and their behavior in making purchase decisions. This removes correlation in the process and builds causality in the real sense. Using a guiding theory like jobs-to-be-done makes the next phase of the entrepreneurial wave far more exciting, while embedding it into the lean start-up concepts. However, with the theory's umbrella concept, the whole of lean testing and development gets a new meaning and hypotheses, building causality in the system from the correlational attributes of customers' buying behavior.

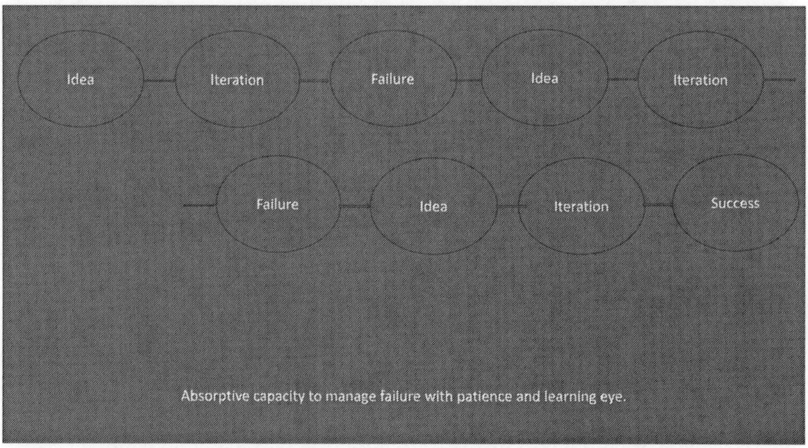


Figure 6-3 Iteration loop in idea development or customer discovery phase

Thus, the founders' teams must balance the skills needed to embed design thinking into idea generation or customer discovery. Normally, finding an ambidextrous entrepreneur is very hard, but building an ambidextrous founding team is possible. Suppose an entrepreneur wants to compete in the existing market rather than creating a new business model entirely. In that case, exploitation of the existing category is recommended where growth is still possible. Building core competence becomes a reality in such a growth phase, so that competitors cannot win the battle. However, focus differentiation, or focus cost leadership, becomes the innovators' focus area where categories are in a slow-growth or declining phase. Having product leadership focused on customer intimacy must be supported by relentless execution capability. As in the saying, ‘culture eats strategy for breakfast’, operational excellence is necessary.

The decision rules in the entrepreneurial world either depend on effectuation (Sarasvathy 2001) logic, bricolage (Baker and Nelson 2005), or opportunity creation practice (Ghezzi 2019), beyond lean startup approaches (LSAs) with the Customer Development Model and lean start-up. As the existing models do not follow balancing exploration and exploitation or effectuation theory or bricolage, implementing such existing LSAs is necessary, but not a sufficient condition for entrepreneurial ventures’ success. As effectuation logic is means-oriented, and causation logic is goal-oriented, balancing these contradictions requires ambidextrous entrepreneurial exploration and exploitation. Apart from the effectuation and opportunity creation view, one needs to think of Lévi-Strauss’s bricolage concept - making do with what is at hand - as an option to manage resource-constrained firms through the recombination of elements at hand for new purposes beyond existing institutional definitions and limits. Baker and Nelson (2005) found this phenomenon in their study, which created ‘something from nothing’ through the use of physical, social, or institutional inputs discarded by other firms.

Opportunity creation vs. discovery theories, when contrasted on cognitive logic, follow effectuation and bricolage and causation. While creation logic is valid for uncertain contexts, discovery logic is valid in risky contexts. In creation logic, LSAs might be the right tools, but in the discovery and causation-driven context, a business plan may be a good tool. However, entrepreneurs do not have choices to follow either. During the product development phase and market development phase alike, one needs to have a balanced view of both creation and discovery logic.

The summary of the discussions above can be shown as in Figure 3. In this process, the guiding theory is jobs-to-be-done. Without losing sight of understanding the causal link between customers’ buying behavior and our product or service attributes, decisions must be carried out. The earlier notions of MVP’s correlational-based understanding will be replaced by MVDP, where the product or service must satisfy the desirability parameter. Ensuring this through multiple in-depth observation, hypothesis testing, and iteration, is the mantra of the next wave of innovation. The guiding document in this process is i4.0BMC; it will follow an elaborate discussion.

On the left side, we have state variables depicting a snapshot of the prevailing condition measured by available resources, such as 'who am I', 'what can I do', and 'whom I know'. Apart from using the resources in tangible or intangible, or in stakeholder's mode, contingencies are part of entrepreneurial life, and leveraging such contingencies in delivering entrepreneurial exploration and exploitation is a must if an entrepreneur wants to succeed. Allocation of these resources is moderated by the decision logic of effectuation, causation, or bricolage. While carrying out exploration-related activities, an entrepreneur needs to use effectuation logic mainly driven by experimentation and observation. But the entrepreneur needs to decide, based on causation logic, if it is entrepreneurial exploitation. Balancing these acts, and using bricolage when necessary, is essential in nurturing entrepreneurial exploration and exploitation, as shown in the box on the right side with change variables.

While conducting the change process through entrepreneurial exploration and exploitation with the help of moderating decision logic of effectuation, causation, and bricolage, the BMOL loop needs to be churned as a flywheel effect, that tests and experiments all hypotheses in leveraging the resources to create a plausible product or service that the customers want through each phase of customer development model or lean start-up model. The ultimate summation of change happening on the right side in Figure 3 is to maximize customer lifetime value, as shown in the state variable on the left side of the diagram, which is also moderated by the decision-making logic in the middle; effectuation, causation, and bricolage. Apart from the internal analysis above, decision-makers must assess the operating environment's industry dynamics. Porter's five forces, and the advent of the complementors in the ecosystem-based or platform-based economy, i4.0, enable many opportunities, as evident from the i4.0BMC and customer validation process in Chapter 4.

Once the customer discovery and customer validation achieve the customers' understanding of the jobs-to-be-done through MVDP and i4.0BMC, the next phase of customer creation and company building starts. However, suppose we recall the discussion in Chapter 1. In that case, it is essential to understand that most startups fail due to the correlational attributes of product or service and the customer's use cases, which results in premature scaling. With the approach suggested by this book, there is a probability that the entrepreneur's vision and art in understanding the jobs-to-be-done, or use cases, makes the scaling at the right time, and with the right product, that customers desire.

However, as shown in Table 1, Porter's six forces in an old and new wave of industrial change are listed, which demonstrates the competitive dynamics, and whether any firms are willing to challenge the existing players in the industry, building competitive supremacy, or, for that matter, competitive supremacy, must start from inception. Some of the key features shown below are important to understand. The competitive dynamics are increasing; substitutes are increasing, buyers and suppliers are gaining bargaining power compared to traditional industries. However, in this new industry, complementors are unique, making all the decision-making challenges, and you are not alone. Still, as an ecosystem, you will survive and flourish.

**Table 1. Modified Porter's Six Forces Analysis for Traditional and Industry 4.0 (source: author)**

| **Forces** | Majority of the industrial age companies | Majority of the Industry 4.0 (i4.0) (Information age companies) |
|---|---|---|
| **The entry of new competitors** | Medium | High |
| **The threat of substitutes** | Low | High |
| **The bargaining power of buyers** | Medium | Very high |
| **The bargaining power of suppliers** | Low | High |
| **The rivalry among the existing competitors** | Medium | Very high |
| **Role of complementors** | None | Very high |

Bertsimas and Thiele (2006) argued for robust and data-driven optimization to solve modern decision-making under uncertainty. Earlier models of decision-making assumed perfect information. However, the inherent nature of uncertainty makes one vulnerable to not having excellent knowledge. If decisions are made with such models, implementation will result in poor performance. What is needed is the analytical framework, which can give results with limited information available. Such a model is anchored in robust and data-driven optimization, which makes the BMOL loop most effective. Therefore, mathematical models have evolved to a greater degree, and merged with AI and machine learning to make them even more effective.

**Revisiting i4.0BMC from the decision-making perspective.**

The 11 elements of i4.0BMC are listed below, and a brief discussion about each element is presented from the eye of the business model SEARCH angle. However, the underlying theory is to match the jobs-to-be-done with the product attributes and solutions to compete against luck in entrepreneurial pursuits where causality rules, not the correlation of attributes. Though it's a repetition from an earlier chapter, we need to make sure that readers can fully understand each chapter in the absence of other chapters. To achieve that goal, the following summary has been reproduced.

1. Key partners
2. Key activities
3. Key resources (metrics)
4. Value proposition
5. Unfair advantages
6. Customer segments
7. Channels
8. Cost structure
9. Revenue structure
10. Social and environmental costs
11. The social and environmental benefit

**Key Partners**. As the new wave will erase many silos inside the organization and across the organization's boundary, key partners will be the cornerstones of the generation of a new business model. These partnerships will be the value-added components to assess the industry's unique problem, which can be solved through strategic alliances, as has been done by the airline industry. There can be a community of cooperation rather than competition. Porter's notion of competitive supremacy is being replaced by cooperative supremacy, where network power and network position determine value creation and capture alike. Ecosystem thinking drives startups from inception, not only with suppliers and distributors, but a partnership with customers could also herald a new wave of customer discovery, validation, and customer creation at the same time. Rather than self-reliance, now the idea is to build inter-reliance.

**Key Activities**. The new dimensions inside this block of i4.0BMC are mainly driven by data analytics to gather, analyze, optimize and go for predictive models in decision-making rather than the prescriptive models of the past. Monitoring and evaluation is something that becomes real-time and more efficient. Asset allocation and management in 5G technologies, sensors, or total architectures, becomes the need of the hour. Rather than waiting for a long time to resolve issues, a new approach to problem-solving becomes a reality.

**Key Resources/Key Metrics**. The significant change unfolding in front of any entrepreneur now revolves around the Industrial Internet of Things (IIoT), real-time sensors with 5G-enabled data transmission links to the cloud-based servers, intellectuals with data science, machine learning, and state of the art after-sales service. While entrepreneurs may think these might be just an evolution of existing IT, their impact in industries and startups is phenomenal. Let us not be blinded by the obvious, but be vigilant in understanding the implications of the unfair advantages firms are making due to the i4.0 technologies and resources. With these metrics and data, the wisdom which the decision-makers have, has surpassed all other revenue streams. Data-as-a-service may become another frontier of the business model.

**Value Proposition/Additional Digital Services**. The i4.0-enabled business model reduces cost and risk, helps build tailored solutions, empowers incremental improvement, has the power of optimization as discussed earlier in the BMOL loop, enhances productivity, builds foresight, and bolsters confidence. Though it sounds like a fairytale, these drive the unfair advantages discussed earlier.

**Channels.** For existing businesses, the existing customer base will be essential, but for new startups, customer discovery and customer validation assumptions are, that with the help of i4.0, entrepreneurs can build repeat business and reputation-based thinking in all phases of MVP testing.

**Customer Segments**. Entrepreneurs have a high chance of transforming industry with their disruptive innovation where the industry is mature enough, and highly competitive with a tight profit margin.

**Cost Structure and Revenue Streams**. Although the cost structure will be performance-driven, upfront investments are needed to trigger the transformation project. The right side of such a transformation or innovation or venture is that subscription business models are feasible, usage-based fees can be charged, and after-sales service can be a revenue stream as well. In earlier transformations, IT only enabled cost efficiency, but in this new transformation, i4.0 enables new revenue and business model streams, which is why the world's best companies are fighting over a pie made out of such a transformative technology and emerging business models.

**Social and Environmental Cost and Benefit**. In traditional business models, entrepreneurs needed to think for differentiation advantage or cost leadership so that sustainable competitive advantage could be achieved. However, in the i4.0 era, the business model itself is built around the unfair advantages created by i4.0. Provided the entrepreneur finds the business model anchored in these unfair advantages, the business is sustainable in the long run, and competition becomes irrelevant.

Everyone is trying to create their 'blue ocean' where there is no cut-throat competition as in the 'red ocean'. Creating a small street and becoming a monopolist in that street is far better than competing on a highway of multiple competitors for the same business model where profit is the main motive. This novelty makes the i4.0 BMC a unique contribution to synthesis from various authors' contributions, as listed in Figure 4.

However, tools and technologies are neither good nor bad in themselves. How the user of the technology uses that technology rests with him/herself. From this perspective, the morality of users of capitalism to keep competition alive as free and fair competition drives innovation, and progress must be safeguarded. Otherwise, the world will lose the thin hope of creative destruction suggested by Schumpeter, and the real tenet of capitalism to correct itself becomes unfeasible.

As briefly outlined under issues and controversies, using effectuation theory in making MVP decisions and pivot or persevere decisions after customer validation means an entrepreneur can use the logic of control. As far as you can control the future outcome, you do not need to predict it. You co-create the future in harmony with the environment with a logic of how much you can afford to lose, rather than the expected return. Rather than focusing on the competitive advantages, the entrepreneur may build competitive models of strategic alliances and partnerships. Rather than exploiting preexisting knowledge to create the future, effectuation logic takes contingencies as given constraints, and empowers entrepreneurs to leverage those contingencies. As said earlier, the entrepreneurial notion needs to embrace the control logic, rather than a prediction of the future. Therefore, affordable loss, acceptable risk, strategic partnerships, and control logic become the four principles based on effectuation theory (Sarasvathy 2001).

In linking the effectuation logic with entrepreneurial exploration and exploitation, entrepreneurs may think that the decisions related to exploration activities must follow effectuation logic. In contrast, decisions related to exploitation-related activities must follow causation models. Thus, in balancing entrepreneurial exploration and exploitation, both effectuation and causation thinking can be utilized. Rather than looking at these dichotomies as either/or, entrepreneurs must embrace 'both' approaches and learn to balance these, as and when the environment and the issues at hand demand. While ambidexterity at the entrepreneurial level would be good, genetics have not contributed to shaping such outcomes in large numbers. Only a small percentage of the population are that breed of ambidextrous entrepreneurs. However, the models and data science available to entrepreneurs through the adoption of i4.0 may mitigate entrepreneurs' weaknesses so that the entrepreneurial level's ambidexterity could be realized. Though implications will be covered in a separate chapter at the end, it is essential to highlight the critical implications of i4.0 research and implementation, together with the impact on globalization, economic nationalism, or populism; the bubble we are witnessing in recent times as triggered by BREXIT and Trumponomics.

## CONCLUSION

The discussions above clearly suggest that the model indicated in Figure 2 could be developed further by building a multilevel model. However, this book's scope does not have space and structure to establish that in full scale. Therefore, further research in creating a comprehensive model at the macro, meso, and micro levels is highly recommended. Yes, CLV has been portrayed as a panacea of all problems, but that optimistic view must be countered in how this change could be implemented at the team level, firm-level, and at the stock exchange level, must be the next phase of research.

As i4.0 is still emerging, the models to optimize such emerging nature of the innovation need to evolve. As it unfolds, the LSAs, augmented with effectuation, bricolage with a broader umbrella of opportunity creation, and discovery logic, need to be developed. However, my approach was limited to the exploration and exploitation lens only. Therefore, further research in building a hypothesis-driven development would be ideal for optimization algorithms to succeed in real-time.

Decision-making on whether to persevere or pivot a product development decision is not an easy task during the customer discovery, validation, and creation phases. LSAs were deprived of theoretical frameworks such as effectuation, bricolage, opportunity creation view, and opportunity discovery view. With the linkages I have suggested, there is an agenda for future research as outlined above. However, understanding the context of decision-making is critical — in a risky environment, causation-based models are relevant, but effectuation-based models are appropriate in an uncertain environment.

## Implications for entrepreneurs or entrepreneurial managers

The new measurement of an outcome of activities and organizational processes through CLV has substantial implications for entrepreneurs and entrepreneurial managers. Entrepreneurs, at last, have found the right metric to measure progress or performance. As discussed above, such an approach to entrepreneurial exploration and exploitation saves money, time, and entrepreneurial energy. It also makes the venture successful in the end if an entrepreneur respects the four benefits (monetary and non-monetary, or intangible). Silicon Valley, the CLV house, implicitly assumed that CLV automatically results in shareholders' and stakeholders' value in the extended horizon. My attempt through this book has been to establish a clear nexus between these three constructs: CLV — shareholders' value maximization — and stakeholders' value maximization. The first link between CLV and shareholders' value has been established, but the connection with stakeholder demands further research to unpack the black box in establishing this nexus.

## Implications for management theories

Shareholder supremacy still rules the world, not only in large companies, but also in the venture capital-based startup world as well. However, this philosophy's peril is that entrepreneurial ventures' failure rate is nine out of ten. As I have attempted to build the nexus with a new dependent variable, it is vital to understand the linkage between CLV and shareholder theory and, later, stakeholder theory if entrepreneurs want to maximize their chances of success and increase it to 3 wins out of 10 entrepreneurial ventures. How stakeholder theory embraces the CLV, however, is a separate book in itself.

**Implications for accounting practices**

The significant implication for the existing accounting practices is that the current measures are not relevant in entrepreneurial pursuits. As evidenced by the IBM story, CLV is becoming the core of accounting practice, albeit slowly, as its results are more than 10-fold better than existing measures of resource allocation and revenue drivers. It is high time to move beyond shareholders' value, and demand the long-term stock exchange (LTSE), initiated by Eric Ries and colleagues, and start using CLV and stakeholders' value maximization as the reporting standard, without forgetting the sustainable development goals (SDGs) demanded by the United Nations (UN).

**REFERENCES**

Baker, T., and Nelson, R. E. (2005). Creating something from nothing: Resource construction through entrepreneurial bricolage. *Administrative Science Quarterly*, *50*(3), 329-366.

Bertsimas, D., and Thiele, A. (2006). Robust and data-driven optimization: modern decision making under uncertainty. In *Models, methods, and applications for creative decision making* (pp. 95-122). INFORMS.

Ghezzi, A. (2019). Digital startups and the adoption and implementation of Lean Startup Approaches Effectuation, Bricolage and Opportunity Creation in practice. *Technological Forecasting and Social Change*, *146*, 945-960.

Kumar, V., Venkatesan, R., Bohling, T., and Beckmann, D. (2008). Practice Prize Report—The power of CLV: Managing CLV at IBM. *Marketing Science*, *27*(4), 585-599.

Marmer, M., Herrmann, B. L., Dogrultan, E., Berman, R., Eesley, C., and Blank, S. (2011). Startup genome report extra: Premature scaling. *Startup Genome*, *10*, 1-56.

Marmer, M., Herrmann, B. L., Dogrultan, E., Berman, R., Eesley, C., and Blank, S. (2011). Startup genome report extra: Premature scaling. *Startup Genome*, *10*, 1-56.

Moore, G. A. (2002). Crossing the Chasm, revised edition. *New York: HarperBusiness Essentials*.

Moore, G. A. (2004). Darwin and the demon: Innovating within established enterprises. *Harvard business review*, *82*(7-8), 86-92.

Moore, G. A. (2007). Dealing with Darwin: How great companies innovate at every phase of their evolution. *Strategic Direction*, *23*(9).

Moore, G. A. (2015). *Zone to win: Organizing to compete in an age of disruption*. Diversion Books.

Paul, K., Elango, B., and Kundu, S. (2019). Social responsibility skepticism: shareholder and stakeholder perspectives. *Social Responsibility Journal*.

Ries, E. (2011). *The lean startup: How today's entrepreneurs use continuous innovation to create radically successful businesses*. Currency.

Sarasvathy, S. D. (2001). Causation and effectuation: Toward a theoretical shift from economic inevitability to entrepreneurial contingency. *Academy of Management Review*, *26*(2), 243-263.

Stahl, H. K., Matzler, K., and Hinterhuber, H. H. (2003). Linking CLV with shareholder value. *Industrial Marketing Management*, *32*(4), 267-279.

## KEY TERMS AND DEFINITIONS

**Effectuation:** Means-driven decision-making logic in opportunity creation assumes experimentation as a method to learn about the unfolding future.

**Causation:** Goal-oriented decision-making logic where planning to utilize existing resources to meet the desired goal is assumed right.

**Bricolage:** Lévi-Strauss's concept bricolage--making do with what is at hand--as an option to manage resource-constrained firms through the recombination of elements at hand for new purposes beyond the existing institutional definitions and limits. Baker and Nelson (2005) found this phenomenon in their study, which created something from nothing through the use of physical, social, or institutional inputs discarded by other firms.

**SRS**. Social responsibility skepticism is a new construct encompassing what makes one skeptical of a firm's social responsibility.

**STEP. The** Stakeholder-emphasizing perspective of the entrepreneur respects all players connected in the value creation and value appropriation process.

**SHEP.** The shareholder-emphasizing perspective takes a narrow perspective of entrepreneurs that only investors are essential for the firm.

# CHAPTER 7

# ENTREPRENEURIAL EXPLORATION AND EXPLOITATION: BUSINESS MODEL EXECUTION PHASE I


**ABSTRACT**

*Customer creation is a prime concern during the business model execution phase, followed by scaling up, or company building. During the customer creation phase, entrepreneurial exploration and exploitation as a dynamic capability to create sustainable competitive advantage is the new frontier of research in the i4.0 era. Though i4.0-related instruments to measure such a capability are not yet available, this book utilizes an existing example of big data analytics (BDA) as a dynamic capability instrument to measure its impact on firm performance. If BDA alone changes the locus of competition and performance, the combined effect of adopting all i4.0 technologies will have an exponential impact on firms' performance. With the current pace of investments ongoing in i4.0 technologies, a new wave of management paradigm enabled by new business models is emerging. Now, research is needed on how to make sure that such investments are driven by differentiation advantage and cost leadership at the same time. This is possible by balancing both exploration and exploitation to nurture new smart products while investing in quality and productivity. Neither efficiency and effectiveness, nor efficiency and innovation, can afford to be a trade-off anymore.*



Keywords: Dynamic Capability, Big data analytics, i4.0, Sustainable competitive advantage.

## INTRODUCTION

### Impact of customer lifetime value

When entrepreneurial exploration or exploitation starts in a venture, balancing these dichotomies is an ardent task, as discussed earlier. This demands the entrepreneur's deliberate attention to reorient organization whenever it goes beyond the limit of either exploration or exploitation. To manage these conflicting activities, startups are increasingly using customer lifetime value (CLV) as their outcome variable, which measures the sustainable progress compared to performance indicators in large companies such as profit and return on assets (ROA). Though I have been discussing the outcome variable in earlier phases of customer development, it becomes particularly important at this stage.

This approach keeps a customer-first philosophy in their DNA. In contrast, the ROA approach focuses on shareholder's value maximization or profit maximization at any cost to the environment and society at large. For startups also, there is no excuse for not considering shareholder value maximization as an ultimate goal, or even a better indicator of stakeholder's value maximization, but the path to that audacious goal demands disciplined execution driven by customer intimacy to deliver product or service differentiation.

The art of balance, as discussed above, needs multilevel thinking at the firms' level, team level, and individual level as well.

Having a customer-first philosophy at the firms' level is mandatory, but the founders and the product and customer teams must have the mindset and the art (not only the science) of managing ambidextrous (both exploration and exploitation) activities simultaneously. Based on my observations in the startups with which I got involved, the majority of workers have difficulties in multi-tasking. But recently, a trend is increasing for training employees to work in all functions during the early phase of the startup, building cross-functional understanding. Thus, job rotation, not only inside the function, but also in cross-functional teams, is highly recommended. The inherent tension between engineering and marketing gets dissolved through multi-stack workers in technology startups, or product teams and marketing teams in other non-technical product and service startups. However, the latter are becoming things of the past, as industry 4.0 (i4.0) is inherently introducing smartness, automation, cloud computing, and efficiency-driven technologies in any product or company of concern.

The approach taken to build ambidextrous teams may take time, attention, and guidance, from the founders in the short-term, but the first validated learning of the mindset would propel the startup to the next level of innovation and agility in the long-term. When such teams are built to empathize with each other's goals and priorities, the tension created by the conflicting goals of short-term profit versus long-term stakeholder value maximization fades away — and the culture, or art, of balancing entrepreneurial exploration and exploitation flourishes.

In the startup world, the BM*O*L loop is executed speedily to make competition irrelevant. But in large multinationals, entrepreneurial exploration and exploitation have a different twist. In i4.0, the emergence of digital platforms ecosystems (DPE) is the synonym for value creation and value capture space, which challenges the underlying assumptions of existing international business theories such as internalization theory (Nambisan, Zahra, and Luo 2019). Similarly, practitioners need to be aware that the venue for value creation and capture is at the older firms' boundary. Porter's economics, based on competitive supremacy, turns to become cooperative supremacy. The competition world brings all stakeholders into one space, giving rise to stakeholders' reality of value maximization departing from the old paradigm of shareholder value maximization. Therefore, a new model of scaling up entrepreneurial ventures is needed.

## BACKGROUND

The assumptions of customer-first philosophy come from the logic that if we can satisfy customers' needs and become loyal, the customer's lifetime value for the startup is very high. In this notion, customer loyalty and satisfaction are already thoughtfully considered. However, suppose entrepreneurs are only looking for short-term profit. In that case, they may be blinded by the obvious, by not focusing on new product development and innovation, thereby undermining the startup's success in the long-term. Thus, balancing entrepreneurial exploration and exploitation to optimize CLV becomes the first lofty goal, ensuring shareholders' value maximization in the second horizon, and finally reaching the stakeholders' value maximization in the third horizon, if we observe the three circles as in Figure 1.

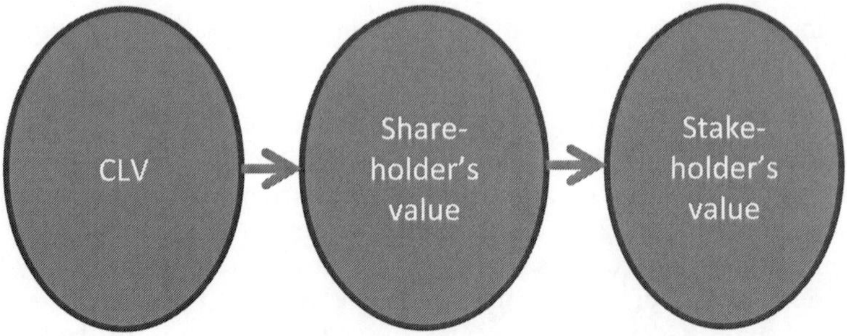


Figure 7-1 Linking customer lifetime value, shareholder's value, and stakeholder's value (Author's conceptualization based on Stahl et al. (2003)

Stahl et al. (2003) argue that CLV is becoming a crucial outcome variable to maintain long-term profitable customer relationships. It is the most valued driver in customer acquisition and retention decisions. However, how the customer-first philosophy brings value to shareholders and stakeholders is still in the research phase. Based on Stahl et al. (2003), there are four CLV components: base potential, growth potential, networking potential, and learning potential. The base potential is estimated through the cashflow generated from the core of the relationship. At the same time, if entrepreneurs can cross-sell and up-brand, it is called growth potential. Similarly, networking potential is generated through the customer's word-of-mouth and referrals; but the cashflow from the knowledge created through the interaction within the relationship becomes the learning potential. The four prospects thus drive the CLV.

CLV is highly important, but the existing accounting systems are not focused on customers, and revenue and costs are not allocated to each customer but instead to functions and regions. Even if we give costs to each customer account, and follow receivables for each customer, how to estimate the non-monetary benefits is not clear. Usually, profit and loss accounts think over a year, or even in quarters, but CLV, as in the name itself, discusses the whole life span of customer relationships, which may be longer than 3 or 5 years. Therefore, if an entrepreneur wants to calculate CLV, he needs to build a separate accounting system other than that used in annual reports. In that case, the startup not only allocates cost and revenue to each customer account, it also captures all four dimensions (base, growth, networking, and learning potentials) through Net Present Value (NPV) of future cashflows plus an estimation of relationship risks (Stahl et al. 2003).

Kumar et al. (2008) illustrate the International Business Machine (IBM) case, using CLV to indicate customer profitability and allocation of marketing resources. The resource allocation and revenue benefits of IBM's pilot study conducted for about 35,000 customers, using CLV, were in the range of $20 million (a tenfold increase) without any changes in marketing investment level. This differential impact makes us think that startups and large firms have so far optimized their processes and activities with a bad outcome variable. Thus, it is not only startups, but also large companies which are also gearing towards CLV. However, my argument is that CLV is highly important in entrepreneurial pursuits in startups and large multinationals. In balancing exploration and exploitation in an entrepreneurial venture, the resource allocation, customer acquisition, and retention, are highly susceptible to existing metrics of ROA or other metrics, which Ries (2010) called vanity metrics, suggesting that innovation accounting needs to be adopted. Thus, using CLV as an optimization variable for all inputs would be highly important.

As the firm's growth is the primary concern at this stage of company development, most companies fail in not being able to cross-the-chasm, i.e. go beyond specific sales cycles. This is a harsh reality in most entrepreneurial ventures. Either they are not ready for scaling up, or they are too late for that. Tuning in to the right time frame to scale up the organization is a daunting task. The majority of serial entrepreneurs rely on the wisdom of their venture capitalist (VC) pairs, but most of the time, even the intuitive experts in each industry get it wrong. Before getting into this phase, as discussed in Chapter 5, pivot or persevere decisions with BM*O*L loops must be done rigorously. Recently, triggered changes due to i4.0 technologies in the product itself, and the companies' business models, demand that we see the firm as a platform, and nurturing ecosystem-specific advantages (ESAs) is necessary. In the following sections, issues, controversies, and problems, of moving from firm-specific benefits to ecosystem-based advantages are discussed.

## CUSTOMER CREATION, EARLY INTERNATIONALIZATION, AND THE BUSINESS MODEL CANVAS

### Issues, Controversies, Problems

As the phase for pivot or persevere ends in the customer development model, customer creation and internationalization start. As the i4.0-enabled startups' or incumbents' transformation heralds a new International Business (IB) growth, I reviewed the IB literature, which predominantly followed the internalization theory over fifty years, to understand why the multinational firm exists, or for what motives internationalization flourishes. These fifty years were dominated by firm-specific advantages (FSAs) and country-specific advantages (CSAs) as the rationale for going with employment contracts abroad, but not through market contracts, (e.g. licensing).

In the startup world, the build, measure, optimize, and learn (BM*O*L) loop is executed speedily to make competition irrelevant. But in the growth phase of multinationals, entrepreneurial exploration and exploitation have a different twist. In i4.0, the emergence of digital platforms ecosystems (DPE) is the synonym for value creation and value capture, which challenges the underlying assumptions of existing IB theories, such as internalization theory (Nambisan, Zahra, and Luo 2019). Similarly, practitioners need to be aware that the venue for value creation and capture is happening at the older firms' boundary. Porters' economics, based on competitive supremacy, turns to cooperative supremacy. The cooperative world brings all stakeholders into one space, giving rise to stakeholders' reality of value maximization, departing from the old paradigm of shareholder value maximization.

Entrepreneurial exploration in industry 4.0, where the platform economy takes hold, needs upfront investment in a large amount, and many of the exploration bets may not actually be realized. Therefore, it is a risky investment, but at the same time, it may become very successful, as are Google and Apple — examples where the digital platform ecosystem (DPE) is well and running. The once-mighty Nokia had to concede defeat due to the platform strategy undertaken by Google and Apple in the 3G mobile business. Nokia partnered with Microsoft to build an ecosystem around Windows mobile, but that did not succeed. In contrast, Apple and Google built their operating systems, application stores, and a vast developer community. Nokia had to divest the Nokia Mobile Phones (NMP) business to Microsoft itself. Even Bill Gates admitted that this partnership, and losing the mobile operating system coupled with the developer ecosystem, were his biggest regrets while at Microsoft. It is an exciting story to think about how the 'choice' made by Nokia resulted in the failure of the NMP, rather than its attributes (emotions and other notions of management).

As we witnessed how technological shifts triggered the collapse of the giants like Nokia, the new information age triggered by i4.0 technologies will make many giants rethink their business model, product development, and CEOs' attention and i4.0 competence. The technological change in IoT, cloud computing, artificial intelligence (AI), machine learning, robotics, and the business rationale in the 21$^{st}$ century is hitting businesses with a hard hammer, blurring industry boundaries. Therefore, CEOs are required to allocate time and attention to the emerging phenomenon - which is a myopic reality, as many of them are rewarded based on short-term profit gain rather than how many innovative bets they have made over the year — the failing outcry suggested by balancing entrepreneurial exploration and exploitation.

The changing reality of industry boundaries, and the platform economy, triggered by i4.0 and entrepreneurial exploration and exploitation, is only possible through modified i4.BMC. Original businesses and emerging new entrepreneurial ventures may both benefit from building a map of the business model canvas's key components. New additions to the original BMC are social and environmental cost-plus benefits, departing from a dependence on economic cost and benefits or profit motive.

Burmeister, Lüttgens, and Piller (2016) outlined not only the emerging new business models supported by i4.0 and platform-based business models, but also that business model innovation is taking place which is changing the firms' and industry boundaries alike. Creating a business model is easy, but implementation and support for the same is a daunting task. It is a new paradigm, and it is changing everything we know as a business so far. We need new best practices to surf in this sea of change, build new organizational structures to align the difference with the new reality, build necessary tools to analyze, optimize, and understand the technology layer, plus its impact on the firms' business models.

Existing tools and structures are not ready to grasp the change we are discussing. There were no smart products with the intelligence to transmit data to the cloud servers for analysis through data mining or machine learning and AI, nor were there data scientists in organizations. These roles will make the cross-functional, organization-wide change as they have an interface with all the functions to optimize both product and process. Customer service data is real-time, and decision-makers can make immediate corrections if something is not right. At the same time, pursuing entrepreneurial exploration for new ideas that can satisfy customer needs and exploit existing services and products to make a maximum possible profit is possible. Management literature has made multiple contributions on how to achieve the balance between short-term gain and long-term success. However, if we suppose the CEO is i4.0 competent (the first time in the history of management), these two conflicting trade-offs could be reconciled, and innovation and efficiency could go side by side.

The changes suggested by Burmeister et al. (2016) have some exciting implications for management theory and practice. The new wave offers the possibility for customization of products and services and efficiency optimization at the same time. This will give an edge to those who understand the meaning of adaptation to individual customer needs. Porter's idea of competitive supremacy based on either cost leadership or differentiation is no more valid. The new change wave will delete the concept of 'stuck-in-the-middle' syndrome while pursuing both cost leadership and differentiation. The old idea of 'red ocean'-based cut-throat competition is no more valid, while the new 'blue ocean' thinking, where competition is irrelevant, is becoming a reality. As business level thinking is changing, so does functional level thinking — balancing the trade-off between novelty-centricity and efficiency-centricity (Zott and Amit 2007) in business model design is becoming a reality, illustrated by Burmeister et al. (2016) using multiple cases. Thus, both entrepreneurial exploration and exploitation are possible at the same time.

The research frontier calling for researchers in this domain is still in its infancy. A new innovative business model, efficiency projects, and implications for theory and research of management are on the verge of emergence. We need to understand the relationships between business model alternatives, competitive strategy, and the resulting performance outcomes in the new industrial internet wave (Burmeister et al. 2016). While I am teaching, I use straightforward existing communication channels like Facebook Messenger to communicate with students (customers). This almost real-time communication has enhanced learning skills, and customer satisfaction levels, and helped build brand ambassadors for the university. Imagine the future classroom, online learning materials, and connected universities in real-time, delivering a new experience to the classroom and learning solutions. If it is happening in the service sector, sensor-enabled products' power will revolutionize the customer experience — even though we need to fix privacy issues at its core. Changes in distribution channels and customer relations empowered by bots and AI will be the new frontier in understanding the customer better and saving costs, simultaneously.

Burmeister et al. (2016) argued that the concept of B2B is changing into B2B2C as manufacturers are getting live data from smart products directly, and the new platform business is already knocking on the door of customers. For companies, embracing the open business model suggested by Chesbrough (2006) might be a good strategy, as networks and platforms with blurred boundaries will be a new reality.

Nambisan et al. (2019) suggested that the DPE is becoming a place for multifaceted innovation, and a multisided marketplace triggered by the wave of i4.0. This makes possible the new ways of scaling up locally and internationally, paving the way for of building knowledge and relationships, and new routes to value creation and delivery. Thus, ecosystem-specific advantages (ESAs) will be the critical factors for the success of companies which are born global, or those undergoing stage-wise internationalization to become multinationals, through a balancing act between entrepreneurial exploration and exploitation. This has implications for the older paradigm called Ownership, Location, and Internalization (OLI) advantages, where firm-specific advantages (FSAs) were the main factors for the reasons for internationalization.

However, entrepreneurial exploration and exploitation logics and rules are different, as we have to move away from FSAs to ESAs in the platform business. Thus, it is vital to understand how ESA logic differs from traditional OLI or FSA logic of the growth of the company. However, researchers must not forget firm-specific advantages and country-specific factors (CSFs). There will be platform openness, modularity, and network effects (Parker and Van Alstyne 2018, Zhu and Iansiti 2012). Such a phenomenon gives rise to the need for ecosystem-specific advantages that are more suitable than firm-specific advantages.

However, the ‘old school’ may argue that, as the firm’s boundary is blurred, we may still call them firm-specific advantages. In this conceptualization, old and new FSA concepts will be difficult to justify. Instead, it is easier to go for ESAs. Though not a strict focus on the moderating effects of many macro and micro-level variables, it is noteworthy to mention that these FSAs, CSFs, ESAs, and context-specific advantages (CSAs) have better performance effects, measured as CLTV, in the presence of favoring market competition, institutional and cultural diversity, policies and regulations, and national/regional standards. The summary of differing advantages and their impact on firms’ performance is shown in Figure 1.

## SOLUTIONS AND RECOMMENDATIONS

### Business Model Innovation Process

In the past, my own experience in the multinational and startup worlds infers that the business model innovation (BMI) process generally resides with the product development department or team. The changing reality of i4.0 triggered innovation is not restricted only to the single product level or department. This demands that the BMI process must be run at CEO or top management team level. It crosses all boundaries (inside or outside) and needs partnerships and alliances, moving away from competitive supremacy to competitive supremacy where all stakeholders are respected. Customer-shared value (CSV) (Porter & Kramer 2011) is possible.

The idea behind the separation of business model innovation and product development is based on the logic that traditional product development processes follow stage-gate processes. In the new era, BMI needs to follow agile, lean start-up, customer development, iteration, scrum design thinking, and hypothesis-based development. This demands flexibility and market-relatedness, experimentation, learning, and optimization loops (Burmeister et al. 2016).

### Entrepreneurial Exploration

At the heart of this change is the possibility for simultaneous pursuits of opportunity discovery and creation, which has divided academicians for over a decade. While building open innovation models with customers and partners, the exploration crosses the firm and industry boundaries. Who knew a social network like Facebook could get into the money business (through Libra)? Similarly, value creation is happening at a high rate of supported competence in i4.0 technologies in the firm, from the top to the factory floor.

The literature on BMC has evolved since Osterwalder (2010), as shown in Figure 2. LEAN STACK popularized the running lean approach through the lean canvas. However, academic literature explored the concept further to develop an outcome-based BMC (Gierej 2017). However, the model suffers from the need to adjust to the social and environmental costs and benefits. Therefore, the modified model is called i4.0 Business Model Canvas (i4.0BMC). The key components are described below:

**Execution of the business model**. The i4.0 business model is fixed for further implementation and execution to exploit the customer creation phase's revenue potential. However, as discussed earlier, as the i4.0-related business model evolves inside the boxes of Figure 2, the boxes remain almost the same. The only issue entrepreneurs cannot overlook is that the boundary of innovation and the firm itself is fragile. Earlier concepts of the value chain are being replaced with value networks.

Similarly, businesses optimized in short-term stock exchanges like NYSE and NASDAQ are being replaced by Long Term Stock Exchanges. The earlier notion of merely making profit is being replaced with social and environmental benefits. Yes, shareholder value maximization still drives the business world; the entrepreneur is thinking through more sustainable development goals (SDGs) and perspectives recommended by the United Nations. While Greta (Thunberg) is bunking classes to raise awareness of climate change, new waves of entrepreneurs embrace the reality of climate and society first, and profit second. A new era is being formed in front of our eyes, where the future is shaping up inside the cloud-based-algorithm-optimized (CBAO) solutions.

The 11 elements of i4.0BMC are listed below, and a brief discussion about each component is presented from the business model execution angle. However, the underlying theory is to match the jobs-to-be-done with the product attributes and solutions to compete against luck in entrepreneurial pursuits where causality rules, not the correlation of attributes. Though it's a repetition to some level from an earlier chapter, we need to make sure that readers can fully understand each chapter in the absence of other chapters. In the following paragraphs, a summary of the business model canvas from the growth phase perspectives is outlined for the readers to grasp the essence of the business model's evolving nature.

1. Key partners
2. Key activities
3. Key rcsources (metrics)
4. Value proposition
5. Unfair advantages
6. Customer segments
7. Channels
8. Cost structure
9. Revenue structure
10. Social and environmental costs
11. The social and environmental benefit

**Key Partners**. As the new wave will erase many silos inside the organization and across the organization's boundary, key partners will be the cornerstones of the generation of a new business model. These partnerships will be the value-added components to assess the industry's unique problem, which could be solved through strategic alliances as has been seen in the airline industry. There can be a community of cooperation rather than competition. Porter's notion of competitive supremacy is being replaced by cooperative supremacy, where network power and network position determine value creation and capture alike. Ecosystem thinking drives startups from inception. A partnership not only with suppliers and distributors, but with customers, could also herald a new wave of customer discovery, validation, and customer creation at the same time. Rather than self-reliance, the idea now is to build inter-reliance.

**Key Activities**. The new dimensions inside this block of i4.0BMC are mainly driven by data analytics to gather, analyze, optimize, and go for predictive models in decision-making rather than prescriptive models in the past. Monitoring and evaluation is something that becomes real-time and more efficient. Asset allocation and management in 5G technologies or sensors or total architectures becomes the need of the hour. Rather than waiting for a long time to resolve issues, a new approach to problem-solving becomes a reality.

**Key Resources/Key Metrics**. The significant change unfolding in front of any entrepreneur now revolves around the Industrial Internet of Things (IIoT), real-time sensors with 5G-enabled data transmission links to cloud-based servers, intellectuals with data science machine learning, and state-of-the-art after-sales service. While entrepreneurs may think these might be just an evolution of existing IT, its impact in industries and startups is phenomenal. Let us not be blinded by the obvious, but be vigilant in understanding the implications of the unfair advantages firms are creating due to the i4.0 technologies and resources. With these metrics and data, the wisdom the decision-makers have, surpasses all other revenue streams. Data-as-a-service may become another frontier of the business model.

**Value Proposition/Additional Digital Services**. The i4.0-enabled business model reduces cost and risk, and helps build tailored solutions. It empowers incremental improvement, has the power of optimization as discussed earlier in the BMOL loop, enhances productivity, builds foresight, and bolsters confidence. Though it sounds like a fairytale, these drive the unfair advantages discussed earlier.

**Channels**. For existing businesses, the existing customer base will be essential. Still, for new startups, the customer discovery and customer validation assumptions are, that with the help of i4.0, entrepreneurs can build repeat business and reputation-based thinking in all MVP testing phases.

**Customer Segments**. Entrepreneurs have a high chance of transforming industry with their disruptive innovation where the industry is mature enough, and highly competitive with a tight profit margin.

**Cost Structure and Revenue Streams**. Although the cost structure will be performance-driven, upfront investments are needed to trigger the transformation project. The right side of such a transformation or innovation or venture is that subscription business models are feasible, usage-based fees could be charged, and after-sales service could also be a revenue stream. In earlier transformations, IT only enabled cost efficiency. In this new transformation, i4.0 helps new revenue and business model streams, which is the reason the world's best companies are fighting over a pie made out of such transformative technology and emerging business models.

**Social and Environmental Cost and Benefit**. In traditional business models, entrepreneurs needed to think for differentiation advantage or cost leadership so that sustainable competitive advantage could be achieved. However, in the i4.0 era, the business model itself is built around the unfair advantages created by i4.0. Provided the entrepreneur finds the business model anchored in these unfair advantages, the business is sustainable in the long run, and competition becomes irrelevant.

Everyone is trying to create their 'blue ocean' where there is no cut-throat competition in the 'red ocean'. Creating a small street and becoming a monopolist in that street is far better than competing on a highway of multiple competitors for the same business model where profit is the main motive. This novelty makes the i4.0 BMC a unique contribution to synthesis from various authors' contributions, as listed in Figure 4.

However, tools and technologies are neither good nor bad in themselves. How the user of the technology uses that technology rests on the user him/herself. In this perspective, the morality of the users of capitalism to keep competition alive as free and fair competition drives innovation, and progress must be safeguarded. Otherwise, the world will lose the thin hope of creative destruction suggested by Schumpeter, and the fundamental tenets of capitalism to correct itself becomes unfeasible.

As briefly outlined in the issues and controversies, using effectuation theory in making MVP decisions and pivot or persevere decisions after the customer validation - the logic of control - can be used. As far as you can control the future outcome, you do not need to predict it. You co-create the future in harmony with the environment with the logic of how much you can afford to lose, rather than expected return. Rather than focusing on the competitive advantages, the entrepreneur may build competitive models of strategic alliances and partnerships. Rather than exploiting the preexisting knowledge to create the future, effectuation logic takes contingencies as given constraints and empowers entrepreneurs to leverage those contingencies. As said earlier, the entrepreneurial notion needs to embrace the control logic rather than a prediction of the future. Therefore, affordable loss, acceptable risk, strategic partnerships, and the sense of control become four principles based on effectuation theory (Sarasvathy 2001).

In linking effectuation logic with entrepreneurial exploration and exploitation, entrepreneurs may think that the decisions related to exploration activities must follow effectuation logic. In contrast, decisions related to exploitation-related activities must follow causation models. Thus, in balancing entrepreneurial exploration and exploitation, both effectuation and causation thinking can be utilized. Rather than looking at these dichotomies as either/or, entrepreneurs must embrace 'both' approaches and learn to balance these, as and when the environment and the issues at hand demand. While ambidexterity at the entrepreneurial level would be good, genetics have not contributed to shaping such outcomes in a large number. Only a small percentage of the population are that breeds of ambidextrous entrepreneur. However, the models and data science available to entrepreneurs through the adoption of i4.0 may mitigate an entrepreneur's weaknesses to realize the entrepreneurial level's ambidexterity.

Though implications will be covered in a separate chapter at the end, it is essential to highlight the critical implications of i4.0 research and implementation, together with the impact on globalization, economic nationalism, or populism — the bubble we are witnessing in recent times as triggered by BREXIT and Trumponomics.

## Entrepreneurial Exploitation

Over the years, the nurturing of ICT- benefitted efficiency projects; however, it will be different this time. While leveraging optimization algorithms in the manufacturing and resource allocation, the vast benefits come from the new ideas and processes that may become the cornerstone of competitive advantage, or, for that matter, sustainable advantages where all stakeholders benefit from each other. To succeed, a new culture of experimentation, celebrating failure for learning, and meritocracy based on i4.0 skills, must be the focus of the culture, as 'culture eats strategy for breakfast'.

Nambisan et al. (2019) suggested that the DPE is becoming a place for multifaceted innovation and a multisided marketplace. This makes possible the new ways of internationalization, new ways of building knowledge and relationships, and new ways of value creation and delivery. Thus, ecosystem-specific advantages (ESAs), as shown in Figure 1, will be the critical factors for the success of the soon-to-be multinationals, or for the incumbent in entrepreneurial exploration or exploitation. It has implications for the older paradigm known as ownership, location, and internalization (OLI), where firm-specific advantages (FSAs) based on competitive supremacy were the main factors for internationalization. Entrepreneurial exploration and exploitation logics and rules are different in the platform business. Thus, it is vital to understand how these logics differ from traditional OLI logics. However, practitioners must not forget firm-specific and country-specific advantages. There will be platform openness, modularity, and network effects (Parker andVan Alstyne 2018, Zhu and Lansiti 2012, Zhu and Liu 2016). Such a phenomenon gives rise to the need for ecosystem-specific advantages that are more suitable than firm-specific advantages. However, the 'old school' may argue that as the firm's boundary is blurred, we may still call these firm-specific advantages. In this conceptualization, old and new FSA concepts will be difficult to justify. Instead, it is easier to go for ESAs. Though not a strict focus on the moderating effects of many macro and micro-level variables, it is noteworthy to mention that these FSAs, country-specific factors (CSFs), ESAs, and context-specific advantages (CSAs) have better performance effect, measured as customer-lifetime value (CLTV), in the presence of favoring market competition, institutional and cultural diversity, policies and regulations, and national/regional standards.

International business (IB) literature has three main focus areas: FSAs and CFAs (Buckley and Casson 1976); emerging ESFs and CSFs (Adner 2017). In the groupings with ESFs and CSFs, a country being important or having ownership advantages under old OLI paradigms is, mostly, less critical than the ecosystem and context. In this book, our focus is to observe this phenomenon from the lens of entrepreneurial exploration and exploitation. Capturing company, country, context, and ecosystem-based advantages (CCCE) is the need of the hour to optimize customer lifetime value (CLV), as shown in Figure 1. The majority of the platform-businesses in the ICT sector rely on giving products or services freely to consumers, and pushing advertising as a source of income through companies or individuals who would like to market their product or brand. In this logic, the privacy of data or content created by users is becoming primarily the source of income indirectly, and outcries over privacy issues, such as that made by Facebook through Cambridge Analytica, is paramount.

As already mentioned, the new locus of innovation, search, and exploration has shifted into the firms' boundaries with collaboration and competition with other stakeholders. The same is happening in creating competitive supremacy to exploit the value created through these interfaces, new data-driven business models, and the customer-focus.

## Growth Hacking

Conway and Hemphill's (2019) growth model search and execution is an exciting approach. This model is suitable when the business model execution phase's customer creation phase is ongoing. Revisiting the same model in growth phase II would be interesting in linking the portfolio approach of decision making for growth (see the following Chapter 7). The model is based on an approach of generating growth using a sample from UK technology sectors. The keyword used in the paper is 'growth-hacking', which, according to the authors, is a 'data-informed' marketing approach. Not only that, the focus on digital marketing makes the approach even more popular and more comfortable to adapt. However, the model is similar in the frame to lean start-up thinking, with 'proof-of-concept' in place of MVP used in lean thinking. Figure 3 shows two distinct phases: the search phase, and the execution phase. The discussion on the search phase occurred in Chapter 4, in the customer validation chapter. In this section, the debate about the execution phase makes sense, as we are in the execution phase of the i4.0BMC.

Yes, it is, more or less, data science-based growth hacking, but it also scans the environment to discover, create, and recognize emerging opportunities before the competitor does. Acquiring people with a sense of the future and deriving the meaning from the data are daunting tasks. Also, it is important not to abandon traditional marketing to fill the vacuum between the physical and digital world. It is a mindset and process to utilize limited resources to scale up technology startups. Some literature also talks about agile marketing for the same or similar concepts. Once the business model is found and validated, it is then a marketing and sales task to replicate it in multiple deals. Building customer loyalty and retention, the referral framework, and, if possible, a push for virality, is the first choice, but other techniques in SVP cannot be ruled out. You may go for sticky or paid growth as well.

**AARRR Model: Acquisition, Activation, Retention, Referral, Revenue.** McClure (2007) introduced startup metrics as AARRR. During the marketing and sales process, customer acquisition becomes the challenge of an organization. However, only a few customers activate, visit the website, and sign up to the system or service the startup is offering. Not all of the signed customers will be retained. A startup's challenge is to ensure that the service exceeds its customers' expectations at every touchpoint. Once current customers are retained, a fraction of them will like and refer the service, and make it accessible to everyone else through social media channels. This endorsement causes the company to gain new growth. However, referral alone does not solve the income equation. Some of these referred customers need to buy the product or service to generate revenue.

In summary:

**Acquisition:** Users come to the site from various channels.

**Activation:** User enjoys first visit; a 'happy' user experience

**Retention:** Users come back, and visit the site multiple times.

**Referral:** Users like the product enough to refer others.

**Revenue:** Users conduct some monetization behavior.

**Implications for entrepreneurs or entrepreneurial managers:** The new measurement of the outcome of activities and organizational processes through CLV substantially impacts entrepreneurs and entrepreneurial managers. Entrepreneurs, at last, have found the right metric to measure progress or performance. As discussed above, such an approach to entrepreneurial exploration and exploitation saves money, time, and entrepreneurial energy. It also makes the venture successful in the end if an entrepreneur respects the four benefits (monetary and non-monetary, or intangible). Silicon Valley, the CLV house, implicitly assumed that CLV automatically results in shareholder value, and stakeholder value in the extended horizon. My attempt through this book has been to establish a clear nexus between these three constructs: CLV, shareholders' value maximization, and stakeholders' value maximization. The first link between CLV and shareholders' value has been established, but the association with the stakeholder demands further research to unpack the 'black box' in establishing this nexus.

**Implications for management theories:** Shareholders' supremacy still rules the world in large companies and the venture capital-based startup world. However, this philosophy's peril is that entrepreneurial ventures' failure rate is nine out of ten. As I have attempted to build the nexus with a new dependent variable, it is crucial to understand the linkage between CLV and shareholder theory and, later, stakeholder theory if entrepreneurs want to maximize their chances of success and increase it to three wins out of ten entrepreneurial ventures. How stakeholder theory embraces the CLV, however, is a separate book in itself.

**Implications for accounting practices:** The existing accounting practices' significant issue is that the current measures are not relevant in entrepreneurial pursuits. As evidenced by the IBM story, CLV is becoming slowly popular but is still not in the annual reporting. It is high time to move beyond shareholders' value, and demand long-term stock exchange (LTSE) initiated by Ries and colleagues, starting by using CLV and stakeholders' value maximization as the reporting standard, without forgetting the sustainable development goals (SDGs) demanded by the United Nations (UN).

## CONCLUSION

The discussions above clearly suggest that the model indicated in Figure 1 could be developed further by building a multilevel model. However, this book's scope does not have space or structure to establish that in full scale. Therefore, further research in creating a comprehensive model at the macro, meso, and micro levels is highly recommended. Yes, CLV has been portrayed as a panacea to all problems, but that optimistic view must be countered by the way this change could be implemented at the team level, firm-level, and at the stock exchange level, which must be the next phase of research. A new wave of research is needed under the umbrella of dynamic capabilities (sensing, seizing, and orchestrating the opportunities) from inception. Balancing exploration and exploitation as a dynamic capability in the context of i4.0 is the next paradigm of research that integrates strategic management and entrepreneurship. A few papers by Teece aim to link the business model with the dynamic capabilities, but not in the context of i4.0.

Customer creation through the lens of entrepreneurial exploration and exploitation suggests that once customer validation is done, and the business model canvas for the creation phase is forwarded, after the pivot or persevere decision, the early internationalization starts. With the nature of the innovation taking place, in the cloud and elsewhere, a startup is a born global company. If it is a multinational, it's a global innovation. In the next chapter we discuss how to scale these validated business model canvases, updated with an environmental and social impact perspective since the original BMC in 2010.

Even though the emerging news of the business model triggered by i4.0, and the related outcome variable of CLV, is a plausible approach while using antecedents such as country, context, company, and ecosystem advantages (CCCE), this model needs to emerge as the business models emerge further when we keep on optimizing the algorithms in the business model. A new outcome variable may arise as well.

## REFERENCES

Burmeister, C., Lüttgens, D., and Piller, F. T. (2016). Business model innovation for Industrie 4.0: why the "Industrial Internet" mandates a new perspective on innovation. *Die Unternehmung*, *70*(2), 124-152.

Conway, T., and Hemphill, T. (2019). Growth hacking is an approach to producing growth amongst UK technology startups: an evaluation. *Journal of Research in Marketing and Entrepreneurship*.

LEAN STACK, https://leanstack.com/lean-canvas/ (retrieved 24.09.2019).

Gupta, M., and George, J. F. (2016). Toward the development of a significant data analytics capability. *Information and Management*, 53(8), 1049-1064.

Osterwalder A. *Business Model Generation: A Handbook for Visionaries, Game Changers, and Challengers*. United States of America, New Jersey: John Wiley and Sons, Inc; 2010.

Kumar, V., Venkatesan, R., Bohling, T., and Beckmann, D. (2008). Practice Prize Report—The power of CLV: Managing CLV at IBM. *Marketing Science*, *27*(4), 585-599.

Nambisan, S., Zahra, A., and Luo, Y. (2019). Global platforms and ecosystems: implications for international business theories. *J. Int. Bus. Stud.*

Porter, M. E., & Kramer, M. R. (2011). Creating shared value: Redefining capitalism and the role of the corporation in society. *Harvard Business Review*, *89*(1/2), 62-77.

Schaefer, D., Walker, J., and Flynn, J. (2017, August). A Data-Driven Business Model Framework for Value Capture in Industry 4.0. In *Advances in Manufacturing Technology XXXI: Proceedings of the 15th International Conference on Manufacturing Research, Incorporating the 32nd National Conference on Manufacturing Research, September 5–7, 2017, University of Greenwich, UK* (Vol. 6, p. 245). IOS Press.

Stahl, H. K., Matzler, K., and Hinterhuber, H. H. (2003). Linking CLV with shareholder value. *Industrial Marketing Management*, *32*(4), 267-279.

Adner, R. (2017). Ecosystem as structure: An actionable construct for strategy. *Journal of Management*, *43*(1), 39-58.

Buckley, P. C., and Casson, M. (1982). MC (1976) *The Future of the Multinational Enterprise*.

Jones, M. V., Coviello, N., and Tang, Y. K. (2011). International entrepreneurship research (1989–2009): a domain ontology and thematic analysis. *Journal of Business Venturing*, *26*(6), 632-659.

Parker, G., and Van Alstyne, M. (2018). Innovation, openness, and platform control. *Management Science*, *64*(7), 3015-3032.

Nambisan, S., Zahra, A., and Luo, Y. (2019). Global platforms and ecosystems: implications for international business theories. *Journal of International Business Studies*.

Teece, D. J. (2014). A dynamic capabilities-based entrepreneurial theory of the multinational enterprise. *Journal of International Business Studies*, *45*(1), 8-37.

Zhu, F., and Iansiti, M. (2012). Entry into platform-based markets. *Strategic Management Journal*, *33*(1), 88-106.

## KEY TERMS AND DEFINITIONS

**FSAs:** Firm-specific Advantages. In IB, it is assumed to be the main reason for the firm's success in international expansion activities' internalization.

**ESFs:** Ecosystem-specific Factors. A new wave in IB enabled by the digital platform ecosystem, ESFs will be the reason for its competitive advantage.

**CSFs**: Country-specific Factors. No matter how boundaryless the i4.0 world would be, each country can have the location, resource, factor endowment, or other similar factors that make the business thrive.

# CHAPTER 8

# ENTREPRENEURIAL EXPLORATION AND EXPLOITATION: BUSINESS MODEL EXECUTION PHASE II


## ABSTRACT

*Premature scaling is the primary reason for company failure while starting up or in corporate venturing. However, with the emergence of i4.0, this has become even more challenging, as we do not know the exact business model or the products' transformation. The preceding chapter touched upon a vital aspect of entrepreneurial growth. In this chapter, an elaborated approach to entrepreneurial growth is carried out. The growth model suggests that having only firm-specific advantages (FSAs) is not sufficient, as argued by international business's traditional internalization theory. As open innovation and platformization are the new norms in the i4.0 era, ecosystem-specific advantages (ESAs), country-specific advantages (CSAs), and context-specific factors (CSFs) are critical in achieving the aspired customer lifetime value (CLV) in the customer creation and company building phase. This is only possible if jobs-to-be-done becomes the guiding mantra in the company. Implications for theory and practice through the entrepreneurial exploration and exploitation lens is presented.*



Keywords: FSAs, CSAs, ESAs, CSFs, CLV

## INTRODUCTION

In the past, entrepreneurial growth was driven by FSAs. FSAs are firm-specific advantages embedded in technology, intellectual property rights (IPRs), reputation, brand image, and country of origin image. These factors are summed up together, to determine whether it is cost-effective to go abroad with an organizational setup or sell the FSAs in the marketplace. This led to the origination of internalization theory (Buckley and Casson 1976), which stands the test of time and is slightly modified in Narula et al.'s (2019) conceptualization. In the latest thinking, the new notion of ESAs has been suggested alongside FSAs. Due to the emergence of platformization and open innovation, the firms' boundaries are changing, as are industry boundaries. The ruling of competitive supremacy has been replaced by cooperative or orchestration capability-based advantage. There are no enemies, rather there are collaborators.

In this beginning of a new era, balancing entrepreneurial exploration and exploitation in the growth phase is a daunting task. On the one hand, the entrepreneur must not abandon the search for another wave of the new business model while capitalizing on the recently found business model to return long invested capital. In pursuing this effort, apart from FSAs and ESAs, CSAs and CSFs are equally important. Where a country offers a grand tax haven for an entrepreneur in a particular segment, it is a blessing in disguise. Similarly, the ease of doing business, low corruption, and an FDI-friendly environment may enable internationalization decisions. Earlier versions of startup discourse only thought of growth hacking as a technique. However, such hacking models do not have a comprehensive view of growth in this chapter. Yes, growth hacking is good, but without understanding how platformization and open innovation will rule the world, entrepreneurs are doomed to fail.

## SOLUTIONS AND RECOMMENDATIONS

As discussed earlier, the SVP approach of sticky growth, viral growth, and paid growth-related hypotheses must be tested, and a chosen growth path must be followed. However, the granularity of growth is not only viral growth. When the customer creation phase is over, as stated in Chapter 4, and the decision made to execute the business model based on Chapter 5, implementation in some part is made in Chapter 6, then the growth and company building phase is a more strategic decision, embedded into the resource-based view, the dynamic capabilities-based view, and internalization theory perspective. At this stage, a company may be thinking of an initial public offering to grow shareholder numbers and valuation. An extended discussion of granular growth based on portfolio momentum, M and A, and market share growth, will be seen below, under solutions and recommendations.

In this chapter, we are revisiting Chapter 6. The framework combining FSAs, CSAs, ESFs, and CSFs, needs to be reviewed. Here, entrepreneurs or entrepreneurial managers must implement the business model validated in earlier phases with a revised business model canvas. The entrepreneurs searched for a business model during the previous steps, but in this phase, it only scaled up the company by implementing the validating business model.

The focus here is to observe this phenomenon through the lens of entrepreneurial exploration and exploitation. As already mentioned, the new locus of innovation, search, and exploration, has shifted into the boundaries of the firm, with collaboration and competition with other stakeholders. The same is happening in creating competitive supremacy to exploit the value created through these interfaces, new data-driven business models, and customer-focus.

However, there is a need for new skills and capabilities to transform from old business concepts to new business models enabled by ESAs and CSAs (context rather than country) (Nambisan et al. 2019), as shown in Figure 1. Thus ecosystem-orchestration as a dynamic capability (Teece 2014) is critical in realizing the aforementioned entrepreneurial exploration and exploitation, which has been studied, albeit differently, in international entrepreneurship (Jones, Coviello, and Tang 2011).

Entrepreneurial exploration in industry 4.0, where the platform economy takes hold, needs upfront investment in large amounts, and many of the exploration bets actually may not be realized. Therefore, it is a risky investment, but at the same time, it may become very successful, as seen with Google and Apple — examples where the digital platform ecosystem (DPE) is well and running. These ecosystems will benefit a lot when 5G technology takes hold in the market. Their services have ubiquitous occurrence in the real-time operation of a business, including applications in medicine. It seems imagination is the only limit to how these technologies will impact our lives and social fabric.

Sandberg, Holmström, and Lyytinen (2020) observed this platformization or servitization from complex adaptive systems (CAS) theory over 40 years. When digitization-enabled products or processes become not only automated, but smart as well, the increased connectivity and dynamism demand major architectural and organizational shifts allowing DPEs where ESAs become most relevant. These connections and interactions trigger a multilevel and nonlinear change in the platform organization with constrained generating procedures (CGPs). The CGPs underplay interaction rules, design control, and stimuli-response variety, making the multilevel and recursive nature of digitally-driven growth in a physical product platform. These changes will transform all product-oriented industries through digitalization/digitization and servitization, which have enabled a service-dominant paradigm.

The once-mighty, Nokia had to concede defeat due to the platform strategy taken by Google and Apple in the 3G mobile business. Nokia partnered with Microsoft to build an ecosystem around Windows mobile, but that did not succeed. In contrast, Apple and Google built their operating systems, application stores, and a vast developer community. Nokia had to divest the Nokia Mobile Phones (NMP) business to Microsoft. Even Bill Gates admitted that this partnership, and losing the mobile operating system coupled with the developer ecosystem, was his biggest regret while at Microsoft. It is a fascinating story to think about how the 'choice' made by Nokia resulted in the failure of NMP, rather than other attributes (emotions and other notions of management).

As a witness to Nokia's phenomenal rise and fall, from the inside, my observation is that it was neither a purely strategic choice problem nor the attribution of shared emotions. Yes, the Nokia board made the wrong decision not to promote an existing capable Finnish cadre to the post of CEO. When Stephen Elop was appointed as CEO, the internal candidate left Nokia, and this departure broke the NMP's 'diamond team' completely. This triggered shared emotions in the lower management and employees. Therefore, it was a mixed effect of strategic choices (the wrong selection of CEO and the wrong choice of the mobile operating system) as well as attribution reasons, which led to the demise of NMP. However, if we look at survival rather than leadership as a dependent variable, the parent company survived well, and turnaround is happening smoothly.

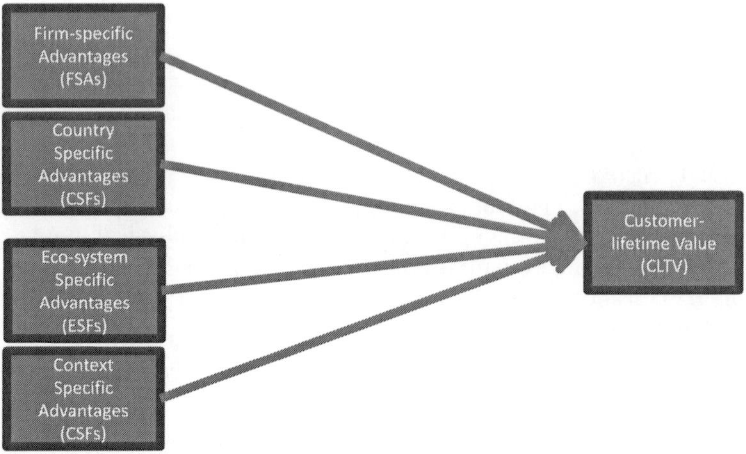


Figure 8-1 Firm, country, ecosystem, and context-specific advantages needed for entrepreneurial exploration and exploitation in industry 4.0 (Author's modification based on Buckley and Casson 1976, Nambisan, Zahra, and Luo 2019, Hennart 1977, 1982, Rugman 1981, Rugman and Verbeke 1992, 2001, 2003, 2004).

It is not only the technological changes in mobile telecommunications, such as 4G and 5G, IoT, cloud computing, AI, machine learning, and robotics, but also the business rationale in the 21st century which is hitting businesses with a hard hammer, blurring industry boundaries. Therefore, CEOs are required to allocate time and attention to the emerging phenomenon — which is a myopic reality, as many of them are rewarded based on short-term profit gain rather than how many innovative bets they have made over the year — the notion suggested by entrepreneurial exploration and exploitation.

The 11 elements of i4.0BMC are listed below, and a brief discussion about each element is presented from the eye of the business model execution angle. However, the underlying theory is to match the jobs-to-be-done with the product attributes and solutions to compete against luck in entrepreneurial pursuits where causality rules, not the correlation of attributes. Though it's a repetition from an earlier chapter, we need to make sure that readers can fully understand each chapter in the absence of other chapters. To achieve that goal, the following summary has been reproduced.

1. Key partners
2. Key activities

3. Essential resources (metrics)
4. Value proposition
5. Unfair advantages
6. Customer segments
7. Channels
8. Cost structure
9. Revenue structure
10. Social and environmental costs
11. The social and environmental benefit

**Key Partners**. As the new wave will erase many silos inside the organization and across the organization's boundary, key partners will be the cornerstones of the generation of a new business model. These partnerships will be the value-added components to assess the industry's unique problem, which could be solved through strategic alliances as seen in the airline industry. There can be a community of cooperation rather than competition. Porter's notion of competitive supremacy is being replaced by cooperative dominance where network power and network position determine value creation and capture alike. Ecosystem thinking drives startups from inception. Partnership, not only with suppliers and distributors, but with customers, could herald a new wave of customer discovery, validation, and customer creation, at the same time. Rather than self-reliance, the idea now is to build inter-reliance.

**Key Activities**. The new dimensions inside this block of i4.0BMC are mainly driven by data analytics to gather, analyze, optimize and go for predictive models in decision making, rather than the prescriptive models of the past. Monitoring and evaluation is something that becomes real-time and more efficient. Asset allocation and management in 5G technologies, sensors, or total architectures, becomes the need of the hour. Rather than waiting for a long time to resolve issues, a new approach to problem-solving becomes a reality.

**Key Resources/Key Metrics**. The significant change unfolding in front of any entrepreneur now revolves around the Industrial Internet of Things (IIoT), real-time sensors with 5G-enabled data transmission links to the cloud-based servers, intellectuals with data science, machine learning, and state-of-the-art after-sales service. While entrepreneurs may think these might just be an evolution of existing IT, its impact in industries and startups is phenomenal. Let us not be blinded by the obvious, but be vigilant in understanding the implications of the unfair advantages firms are creating due to i4.0 technologies and resources. With these metrics and data, the wisdom the decision-makers have, surpasses all other revenue streams. Data-as-a-service may become another frontier of the business model.

**Value Proposition/Additional Digital Services**. The i4.0 enabled business model reduces cost and risk, helps build tailored solutions, empowers incremental improvement, has the power of optimization as discussed earlier in the BMOL loop, enhances productivity, builds foresight, and bolsters confidence. Though it sounds like a fairytale, these drive the unfair advantages discussed earlier.

**Channels**. For existing businesses, the existing customer base will be essential. Still, for new startups, customer discovery and customer validation assumptions are that, with the help of i4.0, entrepreneurs can build repeat business and reputation-based thinking in all phases of MVP testing.

**Customer Segments**. Entrepreneurs have a high chance of transforming industry with their disruptive innovation where the industry is mature enough, and highly competitive with a tight profit margin.

**Cost Structure and Revenue Streams**. Although the cost structure will be performance-driven, upfront investments are needed to trigger the transformation project. The right side of such a transformation or innovation or venture is that subscription business models are feasible, usage-based fees could be charged, and after-sales service could be a revenue stream. In earlier transformations, IT only enabled cost efficiency, but in this new transformation, i4.0 helps new revenue and business model streams, which is the reason the world's best companies are fighting over a pie made out of such transformative technology and emerging business models.

**Social and Environmental Cost and Benefit**. In traditional business models, entrepreneurs needed to think for differentiation advantage or cost leadership so that sustainable competitive advantage could be achieved. However, in the i4.0 era, the business model itself is built around the unfair advantages created by i4.0. Provided the entrepreneur finds the business model anchored in these unfair advantages, the business is sustainable in the long run, and competition becomes irrelevant.

Everyone is trying to create their 'blue ocean' where there is no cut-throat competition in the 'red sea'. Creating a small street and becoming a monopolist in that street is far better than competing on a highway of multiple competitors for the same business model where profit is the main motive. This novelty makes i4.0 BMC a unique contribution to synthesis from various authors' contributions, as listed in Figure 1.

However, tools and technologies are neither good nor bad in themselves. How the user of the technology uses that technology rests on the user him or herself. From this perspective, the morality of users of capitalism to keep competition alive as free and fair competition drives innovation, and progress must be safeguarded. Otherwise, the world will lose the thin hope of creative destruction suggested by Schumpeter, and the fundamental tenet of capitalism to correct itself becomes unfeasible.

As briefly outlined in the issues and controversies, using effectuation theory in making MVP decisions and pivot or persevere decisions after customer validation - the logic of control - can be used. As far as you can control the future outcome, you do not need to predict it. You co-create the future in harmony with the environment with the logic of how much you can afford to lose, rather than expected return. Rather than focusing on the competitive advantages, the entrepreneur may build competitive models of strategic alliances and partnerships. Rather than exploiting pre-existing knowledge to create the future, effectuation logic takes contingencies as given constraints and empowers entrepreneurs to leverage those contingencies. As said earlier, the entrepreneurial notion needs to embrace the control logic rather than a prediction of the future. While ambidexterity at the entrepreneurial level would be good, genetics have not contributed to shaping such outcomes in a large population. Only a small percentage of people are among that breed of ambidextrous entrepreneurs.

Bocken and Geradts (2019) discussed the barriers and drivers to sustainable business model innovation from the perspectives of organization design and dynamic capabilities perspectives, but anchoring discussions in large company contexts. However, when we are in the business model execution phase II of a startup, we need to see how it can move to existing theories and models when the company becomes an SME and, sooner or later, a large corporation. There will be barriers on three levels: the institutional, the strategic, and the operational. Similarly, Zhao, Von Delft, Morgan-Thomas, and Buck (2019) explored the competitive battles in the world of platforms. As discussed earlier in Chapter 4, i4.0 drives the platformization and open innovation; it is customary to pay due respect to the discourse suggested by Zhao et al. (2019). The field of a platform business is under conceptual ambiguity, in need of methodological rigor and analytical approaches. The major shift is moving away from competitive supremacy to competitive supremacy for value creation and capture alike. An elaborated understanding of tension, capabilities, and cognition, as a mechanism to value creation and performance must be considered (Czakon, Srivastava, Le Roy, and Gnyawali 2019). The evidence provided by Zhao et al. (2019) with twelve multi-sided platforms suggests that platform battles are tearing up the limits to entrepreneurial exploration and exploitation. In pursuing platformization, competition is a must, but contingencies that impact competition's pursuits must be addressed in time. Though qualitative research has provided insights in this arena, considerable quantitative research to generalize the findings might be plausible. As it is evident that it has multiple players from multiple levels of analysis, future research must understand the intricate balance between study levels.

Based on the SWOT analysis, testing the critical hypothesis on value propositions and SVP growth (sticky, viral, and paid) using MVP and using AARRR metrics to measure progress is essential. There is an argument that i4.0 BMC will create an unfair advantage for entrepreneurs. How this happens, and how it gets nurtured, is still under research. Entrepreneurial exploration and exploitation will go side-by-side with social and environmental issues. Frolov et al. (2017) delved into sustainable manufacturing within the industrial policy concept of i4.0. Industrial policies are seeing this change as an opportunity for building products and solutions that are competitive in the world market. It is seen that the lag in transformation in interacting with the value chain or, for that matter, value networks, gives a new manufacturing paradigm where innovation and platformization are taking their grip, as discussed in the discovery phase. Even countries relying on old energy sources are realizing that, sooner or later, it is good to move into the renewable energy world and i4.0 world where both innovation and efficiency driven by entrepreneurial exploration and exploitation is a possibility.

According to Blank (2013), business plans usually fail at the first customer contact. However, VCs still demand a business plan. The old notion of running startups as smaller versions of large corporations is a grave mistake in modern entrepreneurial management. To avoid this pitfall, Blank suggested listening to the customers, making the customer-first philosophy a guiding management philosophy. Lean start-up and customer development models are the essential tools available to execute the idea behind listening to the customers emphatically.

Blank (2013) even laid a foundation for the new strategy for corporations where lean start-up becomes a driving process for innovation and entrepreneurship. However, with the advent of i4.0, my model might be more relevant where optimization becomes the critical component rather than anything else. Also, balancing entrepreneurial exploration and exploitation, and related attention in each activity, guide the development process to avoid premature, or too-late scaling. The new wave will make current business models efficient and effective; it will unleash the new business model's power for many years to come where optimization loops give the machine our intelligence, to be better than us in the long run.

While startups follow this technique, future corporations cannot just be observers in the new wave, as innovation must survive. This method might also provide a more significant opportunity as a tool to unleash platformization, servitization, and digitalization. Current schools and colleges are not ready for future skills. There will be educated people remaining unemployed, as they do not have employability in the new age. On the other hand, there will be many new jobs unfulfilled due to a shortage of skills. Some of the AI companies are overhauling this process by providing training. Thus, the old paradigm of execution and efficiency-seeking tools will no more be practical; we need to search for a new business model and scale it up at the right time.

**Growth Hacking**

Conway and Hemphill (2019) discussed generating growth using a sample from UK technology sectors. The keyword used in the paper is 'growth hacking,' which, as according to the authors, is a 'data-informed' marketing approach. Not only that, the focus on digital marketing makes the approach even popular and more comfortable to adapt. However, the model is similar in the frame to lean start-up thinking, with 'proof-of-concept' in place of MVP used in lean thinking.

Yes, it is more or less data science-based growth hacking, but it also scans the environment to discover, create, and recognize, emerging opportunities before the competitor does. Acquiring people with a sense of the future and deriving the meaning from the data are daunting tasks. Also, it is important not to abandon traditional marketing to fill the vacuum between the physical and digital world. Teece et al. (1997) used sensing, seizing, and orchestrating, activities as dynamic capabilities. According to Conway and Hemphill (2019), data science is enabling a new marketing and growth hacking approach, with similar capabilities suggested by Teece et al.

(1997). This hacking also has a similar approach to business model search and execution. While understanding the growth hack, one needs to discover which model will work best out of SVP models. When a vital understanding of either of the SVP models as a growth model is established, the growth model's execution on a large scale happens in this phase of business model execution where customer creation has ended and scaling the company is the focus. However, premature scaling is not an answer.

**AARRR Model: Acquisition, Activation, Retention, Referral, Revenue.** McClure (2007) introduced startup metrics as AARRR. During the marketing and sales process, customer acquisition becomes the challenge of an organization. However, only a few customers activate, visit the website, and sign up to the system or service the startup is offering. Not all the signed customers will be retained. A startup's challenge is to ensure that the service exceeds its customers' expectations at every touchpoint.

Once the current customer is retained, a fraction of them will like and refer the service, and make it accessible to everyone through social media channels. This endorsement causes the company to gain new growth. However, rereferral alone does not solve the income equation. Some of these referred customers need to buy the product or service to generate revenue.

In summary:

**Acquisition:** Users come to the site from various channels.

**Activation:** Users enjoy their first visit – a 'happy' user experience

**Retention:** Users come back, visit the site multiple times.

**Referral:** Users like the product enough to refer others.

**Revenue:** Uses conduct some monetization behavior.

### Granularity of Growth

Baghai, Smit, and Viguerie (2007) argue that there are three approaches to the granularity of growth:

- It starts with portfolio momentum, which is the organic revenue growth of each segment represented in its portfolio. If it's a startup, it may take a longer time to build a segmented portfolio, but for a growing company, this might be visible already. However, taking the organic revenue growth path at the expense of profitability is not recommended, as it does not support the shareholder value.

- M and A is another prong of the three-prong strategy: inorganic growth through buying or selling, meaning acquiring new ventures or divesting non-performing or declining segments.
- Market share performance is another organic growth approach.

In summary, the three-prong strategy could be combined as PMM where P stands for portfolio, M for M and A, and another M for market share. Building a nexus between SVP, PMM, and growth hacking is the most critical aspect in i4.0 era startups' growth trajectory, geared towards balancing both exploration and exploitation, as too little or too much attention in either exploration or exploitation results in failure.

Baghai, Smit, and Viguerie's (2007) findings suggest that focus and growth in organic revenue growth are correlated with the better creation of shareholder value. This approach is one of the recommended approaches compared to M and A and market share growth, as it allows the development of absorptive capacity in the firm. When growth is high, and the company is not ready to serve the customers to its best level to build outstanding loyalty, the viral growth concept cannot be implemented, nor will growth hacking work.

The granularity of growth requires that taking acquisition as a strategy or expanding organically in segments where the firm enjoys portfolio momentum would be the first choice. On the other hand, divestiture could not be ruled out in segments where the firm has good portfolio momentum but is losing market share. The third strategic option could be to acquire a company to build portfolio momentum in slow segments where future growth potential is estimated. Such a portfolio approach in strategic decisions becomes the cornerstone of company building. As stated earlier, at this stage, an IPO could be a plausible option as well. Baghai et al. (2007) concluded that growth decisions need to be granular, and should allocate resources toward businesses, countries, customers, and products, with plenty of headroom for growth.

**Customer Franchise: A new approach to make competition irrelevant**

Unwavering loyalty means you are making a franchise with your customer. Steadfast loyalty is possible if customer service can repeatedly exceed customer expectations (Parasuraman, Berry, and Zeithaml 1991). It shows a continuum of competitive disadvantages to competitive advantage, and the ultimate goal of customer franchising. Viral marketing must aim to achieve the latter stage where customer's perceptions about the product or service the startup is selling exceed the desired level. With this customer delight, the company's future is assured, and jobs-to-be-done theory receives plausible recognition in academia and the practical world.

This is one of the unique approaches in making competition irrelevant when your customer is loyal — no matter what, they will not switch from you. The so-called 'blue ocean' strategy is realized where both value and cost trade-offs are balanced, and a sweet spot to exceed customer expectations is realized. While the rest of the competitors are in the 'red ocean' calculating their market shares, the innovative firm reaps the benefits of the small street it has created and enjoys 100% market share in whatever they are pursuing, through non-consumption jobs-to-be-done logic. Correlational attributes become the decision-making criteria in pivot or persevere loops no longer, they are replaced by multiple causal storyboards tested through MVDP, and the unfair advantages created by i4.0. Let us acknowledge the beginning of a golden era of i4.0 entrepreneurship.

## CONCLUSION

As the research is in the emergent stage, each i4.0 era technology bundle needs separate detailed attention. As an umbrella concept, this chapter attempted to build a model of growth. However, it is a simplified model in that aspect. Dunning's (2000) OLI assumptions must be revisited in the platform economy, locus of open innovation, and concept of IPRs parallel to the open innovation wave. The ruling concepts of the resource-based view, dynamic capabilities-based view, internalization theory perspective, internalization as a staged state, and change variables, need researchers' attention. All of these models are ripe for disruption. Perhaps born global firms will be the norm, rather than the exception.

Departing from the existing notion of FSA-based literature, and linking with the preceding chapter on growth phase I, an elaborated approach to entrepreneurial growth is carried out in this chapter. The model of growth suggests that having only firm-specific advantages (FSAs) is not sufficient, as argued by the traditional internalization theory of international business (Buckley and Casson 1976) but there is a need to embrace the recent conceptualization suggested by Narula et al. (2019). As open innovation and platformization are the new norm in the i4.0 era, ecosystem-specific advantages (ESAs), country-specific advantages (CSAs), and context-specific factors (CSFs) are critical in achieving the aspired customer lifetime value (CLV) in the customer creation and company building phase. Implications for theory and practice through the entrepreneurial exploration and exploitation lens is presented.

## REFERENCES

Baghai, M., Smit, S., and Viguerie, S. P. (2007). The granularity of growth. *The McKinsey Quarterly*, *2*, 41À51.

Bocken, N. M., and Geradts, T. H. (2019). Barriers and drivers to sustainable business model innovation: Organization design and dynamic capabilities. *Long Range Planning*, 101950.

Czakon, W., Srivastava, M. K., Le Roy, F., and Gnyawali, D. (2019). Coopetition Strategies: Critical Issues and Research Directions.

McClure, D. (2007). Startup metrics for pirates: AARRR. *Startup Metrics for Product Marketing and Product Management)*.

Parasuraman, A., Berry, L. L., and Zeithaml, V. A. (1991). Understanding customer expectations of service. *Sloan Management Review*, *32*(3), 39-48.

Sandberg, J., Holmström, J., and Lyytinen, K. (2020). Digitization and Phase Transitions in Platform Organizing Logics: Evidence from the Process Automation Industry. *Management Information Systems Quarterly*, *44*(1), 129-153.

Zhao, Y., Von Delft, S., Morgan-Thomas, A., and Buck, T. (2019). The evolution of platform business models: Exploring competitive battles in the world of platforms. *Long Range Planning*, 101892.

## KEY TERMS AND DEFINITIONS

**FSAs:** Firm-specific Advantages. In IB, it is assumed to be the main reason for the firm's success in international expansion activities' internalization.

**ESFs:** Ecosystem-specific Factors. A new wave in IB enabled by the digital platform ecosystem, ESFs will be the reason for its competitive advantage.

**CSFs**: Country-specific Factors. No matter how boundaryless the i4.0 world would be, each country can have a location, resource, factor endowment, or other similar factors that make the business thrive.

**Growth-hacking**: The approach taken by the marketing team to build a growth model primarily thinking to achieve virality of growth; however other two approaches of sticky growth and paid growth could be tested as well depending on the segment and industry of operation.

**Business model search:** In the early phase of finding product-market fit called business model search.

**Business model execution**: Business model execution is usually followed in the customer creation and company building phase of the customer development model suggested by S. Blank.

**Pirate metrics**: AARRR metrics used in growth hacking or marketing of a startup. AARRR represents acquisition, attention, retention, referral, and revenue.

# CHAPTER 9

# CONCLUSION: IMPLICATIONS FOR POLICY, PRACTICE, AND CAPITALISM WITH MORALITY


**ABSTRACT**

The potential impact of i4.0 for entrepreneurs, entrepreneurship, business and economics, and policy manoeuvring, the development of required skills for practitioners, and implications for capitalism at large, are significant areas of discussion in this chapter, which is derived from the use of the new process, activities, and outcome variable customer lifetime value (CLV). Further to CLV, i4.0's implications for shareholder's value maximization, and hence stakeholder's value maximization, is discussed. While entrepreneurs can feel the gold rush of innovative ideas and opportunities, entrepreneurial processes will go through profound changes, as has been started with this book. Business and economics will never be the same again, with new outcome variables. Mere profit as a measure of success is no longer valid, as social and environmental justice must be included as indicators for future corporations and startups alike. Policymakers need to rage with the machine, not against it. Practitioners must fulfill the skill gap while being creative in their free time, given the gifts of automation. Capitalism must flourish in its truest sense, as a free society. This may be possible for the first time in modern history - all triggered by i4.0.



Keywords: Competition, Innovation, New Skills, Automation, Optimization.

## IMPACT OF CUSTOMER LIFETIME VALUE

Chapter 1 outlined the book's thesis and attempted to set the scene on how industry 4.0 (i4.0) can unleash new business models or develop essential insights for a better decision-making process. It not only includes technologies like 3D printing, IoT, AI, cloud computing, machine learning, robotics, 5G, but also Big Data Analytics (BDA), which is enhancing entrepreneurial exploration and exploitation at its best for solving data challenges, process challenges, and management challenges. i4.0 can enhance value creation and value capture at the same time, with efficiency unmatched so far. First, balancing exploration and exploitation literature is reviewed to build an understanding of extant knowledge. Once this is done, based on the latest literature review on i4.0, a synthesis of the literature's research gap was proposed. Based on this review's research agenda, this book answered a key concern of how entrepreneurs can balance entrepreneurial exploration and exploitation in i4.0. The analytics world is moving beyond descriptive to predictive, and in the future, it will be more prescriptive, enabled by AI, machine learning, expert systems, and 5G. Thus, the future of entrepreneurial exploration and exploitation depends on how information is used to develop an insight to make intelligent, smart, and fact-based decision-making to take actions that may have a real-time correction mechanism and a new wave of quality, productivity, and customer satisfaction, will be a reality.

Chapter 2 took a broader look at i4.0 and entrepreneurial exploration and exploitation. Building a culture of innovation and quality from inception is the right mantra for success. In the earlier conceptualization of the customer development model, and a lean start-up or business model canvas balancing entrepreneurial exploration and exploitation, is not explicit, nor does culture take centre stage in those models. Minimum viable products (MVP) were interpreted as quality compromised products in customer discovery and customer validation. Also, in the age of industry 4.0, these existing models need to be adapted or modified to cater to the changing reality. This chapter outlined the emerging changes and the need for the adapted model(s). Though building product differentiation becomes the core of the entrepreneurial exploration, creating cost savings through entrepreneurial exploitation must not be abandoned. The 'blue ocean' strategy emerges if both balancing of value and cost trade-off are realized.

In Chapter 3, the basic theoretical models were discussed. Entrepreneurial exploration, and balancing the two to search for a new business model and execute the business model extant literature, uses a customer development model, or lean start-up. Departing from earlier literature, we embedded lean start-up concepts into the broader framework of jobs-to-be-done theory (Christensen et al. 2016). Due to the industry 4.0 wave, the change we are envisaging in each industry's business model demands some modifications in the build-measure-learn (BML) loop, which need to be augmented to the build-measure-optimize-learn (BMOL) loop. Even if the optimization was in the model, it was implicit, and the meaning was different. This chapter took optimization as algorithm-based AI and machine learning, that gives real-time adjustments of field parameters so that the possibility to explore and exploit simultaneously is a reality. The entire discourse under the business model canvas shows that the customer development model changes, though we have kept those model's boxes and skeleton almost identical with minor modifications. As discussed in Chapter 2, the book covered how to create relational rent in open innovation and platformization as enabled by i4.0. This change has a massive implication for policymakers and practitioners alike, and academicians may have a perpetual research agenda as the i4.0 evolves further.

## BUSINESS MODEL SEARCH PHASE

Chapter 4 focused on phase I of the business model search. As i4.0 takes off, entrepreneurial exploration and exploitation in the business model search phases can be divided into customer discovery and customer validation phases. However, the guiding theory of jobs-to-be-done says that understanding multiple use cases is a must. The customer discovery phase demands the knowledge of changing locus of innovation and platform economics. This chapter's focus was to link open innovation and platformization in the presence of contingency variables in the potential future firms' performance, estimated as customer lifetime value (CLV). However, the real measure of progress in this phase is validated learning through the multiple iterations of open innovation activities, and platformization efforts inflated or deflated by contingencies in understanding jobs-to-be-done by the customer. Once the customer discovery phase validates some of the assumptions or hypotheses through BMOL testing and measuring the data based on the experiments, the second phase of business model search, called the customer validation phase, starts. In the discovery phase, which was the focus of this chapter, all the interviews and observations were done in blocks of i4.0BMC to test a minimum viable approach. Still, a desirable product (MVDP) or minimum viable concept (MVC) to understand the more significant product or solution that has a causal link with the customer's jobs-to-be-done must be thought through. Such MVDP or MVC reduces the cost of development and failure costs and can compete against luck, as Christensen et al. (2016) suggested. Once the 'learning' in this phrase indicates that the product is feasible, only then does the full prototype or pilot testing of the product start.

Chapter 5 discussed phase II of the business model search. As i4.0 takes off, entrepreneurial exploration and exploitation in the business model search phases can be divided into customer discovery and customer validation phases, as discussed in the previous paragraph. Chapter 4 touched upon the customer discovery phase, while Chapter 5 focused on the customer validation phase where the search is geared towards establishing product-market fit through the i4.0BMC discussed in Chapter 3; the focus on finding out the causal link between the product and service with the jobs-to-be-done by the customer must not be left out. The previous chapter's focus was to link open innovation and platformization in the presence of contingency variables on the potential future firms' performance, estimated as customer lifetime value (CLV). However, the real measure of progress in this phase is validated learning through the multiple iterations of open innovation activities and platformization efforts. In this phase, as in the earlier phase, all the interviews done in all blocks of i4.0BMC will be tested in a minimum viable, but desirable, product (MVDP) or minimum viable concept (MVC) to understand the more significant product or solution we are going to develop. Such MVDP or MVC reduces the cost of development and failure costs as an entrepreneur can iterate on the product or service early enough without burning millions of dollars in the illusion of entrepreneurial vision. MVDP allows entrepreneurs to come to the reality and adjust their vision. Once the 'learning' in this phrase suggests that the product is feasible, only then can full prototype or pilot testing of the product start.

Chapter 6 covered decisions regarding entrepreneurial exploration and exploitation, and the resulting challenge of maintaining the balance thereof demands critical judgment enabled by validated learning of customer discovery and validation. In both phases, the goal was to build a causal understanding of the product and features with the customer's jobs-to-be-done while using the product and feature. If the product-market fit has been realized, the persevere button must be pressed; otherwise, an iterative pivot procedure must be continued. In this chapter, reasons for startup failure and, for that matter, large corporations' new line of business failure (excluding small and medium-sized enterprises) is discussed, and the potential for further research is outlined.

## BUSINESS MODEL EXECUTION PHASE

In Chapter 7, the business model execution phase I was covered. Customer creation is a prime concern during the business model execution phase, followed by scaling up or company building. During the customer creation phase, entrepreneurial exploration and exploitation as a dynamic capability to create sustainable competitive advantage is the new frontier of research in the i4.0 era. Though i4.0-related instruments to measure such a capability are not yet available, this book utilizes the existing example of big data analytics (BDA) as a dynamic capability instrument to measure the impact on firms' performance. If BDA alone changes the locus of competition and performance, the combined effect of adopting all i4.0 technologies will have an exponential effect on firms' performance. With the current pace of investments ongoing in i4.0 technologies, a new wave of management paradigm enabled by new business models is emerging. Now, research is needed on how to make sure that such investments are driven by differentiation advantage and cost leadership at the same time. This is possible by balancing both exploration and exploitation to nurture new smart-products while investing in quality and productivity. Neither efficiency and effectiveness nor efficiency and innovation can afford to be a trade-off anymore. Therefore, constant assessment of the jobs-to-be-done by the customer through products and solutions must be carried out.

In Chapter 8, business model execution phase II is covered. Premature scaling is the primary reason for company failure while starting up, or in corporate venturing. However, with the emergence of i4.0, this has become even more challenging as we do not know the exact business model or the products' transformation. The preceding chapter touched upon an essential aspect of entrepreneurial growth. In this chapter, an elaborated approach to entrepreneurial growth is carried out. The growth model suggests that having only firm-specific advantages (FSAs) is not sufficient, as argued by the international business's traditional internalization theory. As open innovation and platformization are the new norms in the i4.0 era, ecosystem-specific advantages (ESAs), country-specific advantages (CSAs), and context-specific factors (CSFs) are critical in achieving the aspired customer lifetime value (CLV) in customer creation and company building phase. This is only possible if jobs-to-be-done becomes the guiding mantra in the company. Implications for theory and practice from the entrepreneurial exploration and exploitation lens are presented. Apart from measuring CLV's success, social and environmental benefits, such as long-term stock exchange (LTSE) must be measured and must be part of the reporting system in the stock exchange. In pursuing this objective, the nature of opportunity becomes global, and born-global companies will be the norm rather than the exception. When entrepreneurial exploration or exploitation starts in a venture, balancing these dichotomies is an ardent task, as discussed earlier.

This demands the entrepreneur's deliberate attention to reorient organization whenever it goes beyond the limit of either exploration or exploitation. To manage these conflicting activities, startups are increasingly using customer lifetime value (CLV) as their outcome variable, which measures the sustainable progress compared to large company indicators such as profit and ROA. The former approach keeps customer-first philosophy in their DNA. Simultaneously, the latter focuses on shareholder value maximization, or profit maximization, at any cost to the environment and society at large. There is no excuse for not considering shareholder value maximization as an ultimate goal, or even a better indicator of stakeholder's value maximization for startups. Still, the path to that audacious goal demands a discipline of execution driven by customer intimacy to deliver product or service differentiation.

The art of balance, as discussed above, needs multilevel thinking at the firm level, team level, and individual level. Having customer-first philosophy at the firm level is mandatory, but the founders, and the product and customer teams must have the mindset and the art (not only science) of carrying out ambidextrous (both exploration and exploitation) activities simultaneously. The majority of workers have difficulties in multi-tasking based on my observations in startups with which I was involved. But recently, a trend is increasing for training employees to work in all functions during the early phase of the startup, building cross-functional understanding. Thus, job rotation, not only inside the function but also in cross-functional teams, is highly recommended. The inherent tension between engineering and marketing gets dissolved through multi-stack workers in technology startups or product teams, and marketing teams in other non-technical product and service startups. However, the latter are becoming things of the past as industry 4.0 (i4.0) is inherently introducing smartness, automation, cloud computing, and efficiency-driven technologies in any product or company of concern.

There is existing discourse on the coming wave of i4.0 and its implications for free time availability, as work will be automated. The relationship between employment and wages (Mason 2016) will be so significant that a new era's dawn will enable human consciousness to progress to the next level. However, human civilization's absorptive capacity to be free from work, and do more creative things, will be tested for a long-time, as we are not ready to embrace the change and freedom that comes from it. Many societies worship work as their calling, and if it is suddenly taken away, there will be a vacuum. In this chasm, many possibilities created by i4.0 may be curtailed by the resistance to change.

Mason (2016) also argues that the market's price-fixing capacity is eroding as information is freely available in most cases. Similarly, collaborative productions are changing the face of capitalism as we have understood it so far.

The approach taken by this book builds on balancing entrepreneurial exploration and exploitation to build ambidextrous teams, which may take time, attention, and guidance, from the founders in the short-term, but the first validated learning of the mindset would propel the startup to the next level of innovation and agility for the long-term. When such teams are built to empathize with each other's goals and priorities, the tension created by the conflicting goals of short-term profit versus long-term stakeholder's value maximization fades away — and the culture, or art, of balancing entrepreneurial exploration and exploitation, flourishes.

## LINKING CUSTOMER LIFETIME VALUE WITH SHAREHOLDER'S VALUE

### Issues, Controversies, Problems

The assumptions of customer-first philosophy came from the logic that if we can satisfy customer's needs, and the customer becomes loyal, the customer's lifetime value for the startup is very high. In this notion, customer loyalty and satisfaction are already thoughtfully considered. However, suppose entrepreneurs are only looking for short-term profit. In that case, they may be blinded by the obvious in not focusing on new product development and innovation thereof, undermining the startup's success in the long-term. Linking CLV with shareholder value or stakeholder value is shown in Figure 1.

Thus, balancing entrepreneurial exploration and exploitation to optimize CLV becomes the first audacious goal, ensuring shareholder value maximization in the second horizon, and finally reaching the stakeholder value maximization in the third horizon, if we observe the three circles in Figure 1. Going beyond stakeholder value maximization and developing multilevel thinking to fulfil sustainable development goals (SDGs) set by the United Nations (UN) becomes the fourth horizon's focus, as listed below.

**Four Horizon Representation of Figure 1**

**Horizon One:** Innovate with CLV

**Horizon Two:** Seek for shareholder's primacy

**Horizon Three:** Build stakeholder's primacy

**Horizon Four:** Develop multilevel thinking

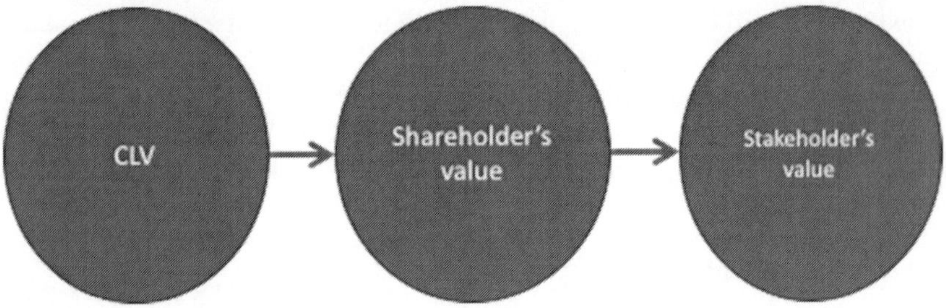


Figure 10-1 Linking customer lifetime value, shareholder's value, and stakeholder's value (Author's conceptualization based on Stahl et al. (2003)

Stahl et al. (2003) argue that CLV is becoming a crucial outcome variable to maintain long-term profitable customer relationships. It is the most valued driver in customer acquisition and retention decisions. However, how the customer-first philosophy brings value to shareholders and stakeholders is still under research. Based on Stahl et al. (2003), there are four components of CLV as shown below:

**Components of Customer Lifetime Value (CLV)**

a. Base potential.
b. Growth potential.
c. Networking potential.
d. Learning potential

The base potential is estimated through the cash flow generated from the core of the relationship. At the same time, if entrepreneurs can cross-sell and up-brand, it is called growth potential. Similarly, networking potential is generated through the customer's word-of-mouth and referrals, but the cash flow from the knowledge created through the relationship's interaction becomes the learning potential. The four potentials thus drive the CLV.

CLV is highly important, but existing accounting systems are not focused on customers, and revenue and costs are not allocated to each customer but to functions and regions. Even if we allocate costs to each customer account, and follow receivables, estimating the non-monetary benefits is not clear. Usually, profit and loss accounts think in terms of a year or even quarterly, but CLV, as its name suggests, discusses the whole life span of a customer relationship, which may be longer than three or five years. Therefore, if an entrepreneur wants to calculate CLV, he needs to build a separate system of accounting other than that used in annual reports, one which not only allocates cost and revenue to each customer account, but also captures all four dimensions (base, growth, networking, and learning potentials) through the net present value (NPV) of future cash flows plus an estimation of relationship risks (Stahl et al. 2003).

Kumar et al. (2008) illustrate the International Business Machine (IBM) case, using CLV to indicate customer profitability and allocation of marketing resources. The resource allocation and revenue benefits of IBM's pilot study, conducted for about 35,000 customers, using CLV, were in the range of $20 million, which is a tenfold increase without any change in marketing investment level. This differential impact makes us think that startups and large firms optimize their processes and activities with wrong outcome variables so far. Thus, it is not only startups, but also large companies, who are gearing towards CLV. However, my argument is that CLV is highly important in entrepreneurial pursuits in startups and large multinationals. In balancing exploration and exploitation in an entrepreneurial venture, resource allocation, customer acquisition, and retention, are all highly susceptible to the existing metrics of ROA or other metrics, which Ries (2010) called vanity metrics, suggesting that innovation accounting needs to be adopted. Thus, using CLV as an optimization variable for all inputs would be highly important.

## IMPLICATIONS FOR ENTREPRENEURS

The 11 elements of i4.0BMC are listed below as a summary:

1. Key activities
2. Essential resources (metrics)
3. Value proposition
4. Unfair advantages
5. Customer segments
6. Channels
7. Cost structure
8. Revenue structure
9. Social and environmental costs
10. The social and environmental benefit

**Social and Environmental Cost and Benefit**. In traditional business models, entrepreneurs needed to think for differentiation advantage or cost leadership so that sustainable competitive advantage could be achieved. However, in the i4.0 era, the business model itself is built around the unfair advantages created by i4.0. Provided the entrepreneur finds the business model anchored in these unfair advantages, the business is sustainable in the long run, and competition becomes irrelevant.

Everyone is trying to create their 'blue ocean' where there is no cut-throat competition, as in the 'red ocean'. Creating a small street and becoming a monopolist in that street is far better than competing on a highway of multiple competitors for the same business model where profit is the main motive. This novelty makes the i4.0 BMC a unique contribution to synthesis from various authors' contributions, as listed in Figure 4.

However, tools and technologies are neither good nor bad in themselves. How the user of the technology uses that technology rests on the user him or herself. In this perspective, the morality of users of capitalism to keep competition alive as free and fair competition drives innovation, and progress must be safeguarded. Otherwise, the world will lose the thin hope of creative destruction suggested by Schumpeter, and the fundamental tenet of capitalism to correct itself becomes unfeasible.

As said earlier, the entrepreneurial notion needs to embrace the control logic rather than a prediction of the future. Therefore, affordable loss, acceptable risk, strategic partnerships, and control logic become four principles based on effectuation theory (Sarasvathy 2001).

In linking the effectuation logic with entrepreneurial exploration and exploitation, entrepreneurs may think that the decisions related to exploration activities must follow effectuation logic. In contrast, decisions related to exploitation-related activities must follow causation models. Thus, in balancing entrepreneurial exploration and exploitation, both effectuation and causation thinking can be utilized. Rather than looking at these dichotomies as either/or, entrepreneurs must embrace 'both' approaches and learn to balance these, as and when the environment and the issues at hand demand. While ambidexterity at the entrepreneurial level would be good, genetics have not contributed to shaping such outcomes in large numbers. Only a small percentage of the population are that breed of ambidextrous entrepreneur. However, the models and data science available to entrepreneurs through the adoption of i4.0 may mitigate an entrepreneur's weaknesses so that the entrepreneurial level's ambidexterity can be realized.

## POLICY IMPLICATIONS: INDUSTRY 4.0 AS AN INNOVATION POLICY DISCOURSE

Significant implications may emerge in balancing innovation policy and competition policy, as the potential for monopoly market is high for the innovating companies because they can collaborate not only with suppliers, but the innovation process may also involve open innovation with customers and consumers alike. This transition is happening so fast that policymakers and machines are competing on who is first. The pending challenge for policymakers is facilitating collaboration across industrial sectors to develop new products and platforms with intelligence embedded into them for data mining and real-time monitoring, and error corrections and prevention. This is a daunting task for policymakers making policies in each industrial sector, as the new frontier of innovation is blurring the industrial boundaries. An example of innovation policy case study of China and Taiwan under i4.0 and sustainability development transition (Lin, Shyu, and Ding 2017) states that the focus must be more on the 'demand-side' policy changes, and the training and competence development of employees and policy-making bodies themselves must be on the agenda for governments and universities.

The globe is being transformed into a village with the Internet of Things (IoT), cloud computing, automation, robotics, and full digitalization of products and processes. Yes, one stream of literature argues that this is the fourth wave of industrialization, which is my assertion. However, a small stream of literature sees the change and metamorphosis as i4.0 policy-driven discourse (Reischauer 2018). Nevertheless, the change will be faster than we anticipated, and we will be in a race against technology and policy change. Perhaps humanity will win at the end, as it has the power to shut down any machines that it creates, unless, and until, we reach technological singularity (Vinge 1993).

## 1. Implications for Business and Economics

For the business world, the implications of information technology affecting our lives have large-scale ramifications. Therefore, it has been called i4.0, meaning the $4^{th}$ industrial revolution. The change will affect work and skills development, economic growth, macroeconomic aspects and sustainability, intelligent manufacturing, and policy related to change and new business processes in cross-value and cross-industry collaboration. Therefore, smart manufacturing and digitalization will become the three pillars of this industrial transformation (Maresova et al. 2018). Earlier the process efficiency used to be the mantra, but now product and process innovation and a new business model transforming the entire industry are possible. Thus, we are entering the world of 'machine intelligence'.

The new measurement of activities and organizational processes through CLV has substantial implications for entrepreneurs and entrepreneurial managers. Entrepreneurs, at last, have found the right metric to measure progress or performance. As discussed above, such an approach to entrepreneurial exploration and exploitation saves money, time, and entrepreneurial energy. It also makes the venture successful in the end if an entrepreneur respects the four benefits (monetary and non-monetary or intangible). Silicon Valley, the CLV house, implicitly assumed that CLV automatically results in shareholder value and stakeholder value in the extended horizon. My attempt through this book has been to establish a clear nexus between these three constructs: CLV, shareholder value maximization, and stakeholder value maximization.

The significant implication for existing accounting practices is that the current measures are not relevant in entrepreneurial pursuits. As evidenced by the IBM story, CLV is becoming a slowly dominant outcome variable, at least internally. It is high time to move beyond shareholder value, and demand long-term stock exchange (LTSE), initiated by Eric Ries and colleagues, to start using CLV and stakeholder value maximization as the reporting standard, without forgetting the sustainable development goals (SDGs) demanded by the United Nations (UN).

Shareholder supremacy still rules the world, not only in large companies but also in the venture capital-based startup world as well.

## 2. Implications for Capitalism with Morality

The coming wave of the industrial internet will be different from the earlier ones, as both efficiency and innovation are possibly triggered by optimization algorithms and transformation of products, business models, and cross-industry collaboration. Post-capitalism (Mason 2019) argues that these changes are possible in three ways: first, as the automation takes hold, there will be reduced need for work; second, the pricing mechanism of the market has been corroded by the information; and third, collaboration is the new form of production and organizing enabled by i4.0 technologies. The early signs of the phenomena are here: alternative currencies, service through time banks, cooperative movements, and self-managed spaces. This transformation has built FAANG (Facebook, Apple, Alibaba, Netflix, and Google)-types of monopolies in a particular sector, and it has given too much power to them. Therefore, in the future, when such monopolies emerge, governments and the public at the same time must save capitalism from the capitalists themselves (Rajan and Zingales 2004) by giving power to the financial markets and free competition. Due to smart, interconnected products and service modules, industry boundaries are blurred, demanding a broader understanding of changing industrial policy dynamics, not based on sectors, but based on a business model incubated inside every innovative, transformative company. This requires a fundamental shift in government officers and companies' ranks, and these emerging competencies are still in infancy. Thus, a rehaul of the curriculum for the longer term, and short training programs for the short-term, are needed.

Capitalism has its correction mechanism, but it has fallen prey to the lobbyists and capitalists without morality. In earlier industrial revolutions, neither the consumer nor the products enabled the business model transformations, but the current wave is just doing that. Some researchers are afraid of singularity; creating technology better than human intelligence (Vinge 1993). This imminent threat demands a proper judgment in technological development and possibilities to strengthen our decision-making capability. We are the product of our choices, not our circumstances. Making the right decisions daily demands human consciousness beyond the current caste, creed, religion, race, and ethnicity. The world is mired into something our forefathers never thought of, even in their lifetime. Our children will not forgive us if we leave the broken world as an inheritance for them — without clean air to breathe or clean water to drink, with natural calamities everywhere, global warming raging a war on natural ecosystems, the chances of mass extinction rising, and the threat of racial and religious wars. The choices we have made so far tell us that it has gone insanely wrong most of the time. Companies are gaining profits at a very high level, but at the cost of social and environmental damage. Thus, every annual report filing to SEC needs to report three bottom lines; profit, social benefits, and environmental impact. Without that, the pollution levels will hit record highs (assuming alternative technological solutions to wipe out pollution will not be here for a foreseeable time). The social fabric will be broken, and environmentally, we will be on the verge of collapse. Thus, the importance of i4.0 technologies to save the planet and social fabric will be of high significance for policymakers and practitioners alike. Let us wake up to the new beginning in search of a new outcome variable!

Emerging changes in technology give power to society (consumers) and make governments able to build surveillance capitalism. If this becomes a reality, policymakers need to consider balancing the power between state and society, as illustrated by *The Narrow Corridor to Liberty* (Acemoglu and Robinson 2018). An organization that respects liberty and freedom of choice flourishes in the long run, but the struggle between state and a liberty-seeking society is always a challenging endeavor. The book *Why Nations Fail* by Acemoglu and Robinson (2012) argues that the real cause of income inequality in today's world depends on the political and economic institutions, including those that support economic prosperity, and extractive which explains the reason for developing nations. For the balancing act of a liberty-driven society and a controlling state, I propose to build a new concept called relative liberty - calculated as the ratio between the degree of liberty in the society, divided by the sum of the degree of liberty and degree of state control. This ratio helps build a measure to plot the narrow corridor (Acemoglu and Robinson, 2018). Too low, or too little, relative liberty is detrimental to society.

Thus, seeking a balance at both ends of the continuum is a must. For aspiring companies looking for a balanced bottom line in economic profit, stable society, and a safe environment, all three fonts' contribution is recommended. Free enterprises thrive where this delicate balance between liberty and state control is a sought-after phenomenon. The new technologies and the emerging business models may have great potential to build sustainable solutions rather than sustainable advantages only; the dogma of the 1980s rules the business world vehemently so far. There is a silver lining in the cloud when the short-term focus thrives in Wall Street and Silicon Valley alike. Most of us think that reinventing Wall Street may be a crazy idea, but it is happening as SEC approves a new Silicon Valley stock-exchange (Franck 2019) called the Long-Term Stock Exchange (LTSE).

Muñiz, Müller, and Kotak (2019) revisited the year-old interview in a Project Syndicate given by Marietje Schaake, International Policy Director of Stanford University's Cyber Policy Center, and a former member of the European Parliament. The discussion concludes that the need for balancing entrepreneurial exploration and exploitation discussed in our book requires an ecosystem of universities and research centres, as suggested by Schaake in an interview taken by Muñiz et al. (2019). This interdisciplinary approach to education, research, and innovation will unleash the power of the best minds in academia and industries alike. Finland built such an ecosystem in the Espoo cluster, near the capital city Helsinki. This cluster houses the Aalto University, the forerunner of open source models, be it software or venture capital and startups. Democratizing startups has just begun. However, this 'overnight' success took a decade or more. After leaving Nokia due to the telecommunication industry's slowdown, I witnessed, as an insider, this vibrant, open-source, model of venture capital, however, recently, as evidence that the capitalists have hijacked this open-source model. Perhaps it will take another student movement to dislodge this capturing and build an open-source venture capital funding and startup scaling model, all driven by volunteers and serial entrepreneurs.

Europe is predominantly driven by free education for its citizens, which is a good starting point to build a professional innovation-oriented research culture where industries support such initiatives with a degree of academic freedom. If this works, perhaps this triangle will unleash demand matching it with supply where a problem-solution fit is obvious. The MVDP costs will be minimal in developing a product and solution to figure out product-market fit and creating a new business model that may hack the existing players' business model. Such disruptions have happened in mobile networks since the emergence of GSM, and now we are in the 5G era, which is unleashing a potential new business model for a decade to come, or beyond.

A fair concern among academics and practitioners is that digitalization and platformization have triggered winner-take-all markets, or caused oligopolistic behavior to flourish. This is detrimental to the core ideology of the Schumpeterian idea of creative destruction when one or two players control the market. Not only will this make the industry stagnant, but innovation and progress in this industry will stall completely. Muñiz et al. (2019) published the views of Marietje Schaake, who is in a school of thought that thinks that the European 'digital single market or space' must not be given up, despite the setbacks of BREXIT and Trumponomics. It needs to support through proper regulation (anti-trust and data regulation) and enable a STEM-based education movement for the brightest minds.

## CONCLUSION

The first link between CLV and shareholder value has been established, but the connection with the stakeholder demands further research to unpack the 'black box' in establishing this nexus. How stakeholder theory embraces the CLV could be a separate book in itself. This new variable may serve the future, combined with SDGs in multilevel models. Similarly, the revised business model canvas will evolve as we learn more about the empirical evidence of using this model. Thus, opening a new frontier of research where models get refined one after another, is best suited for business sectors or industrial clusters which are still unknown. Linking CLV with shareholder value, stakeholder worth, and SDGs, is a logical chain in a four-horizon framework that guides both practice and policy. I have just opened a 'Pandora's box' where the need for a new dependent variable is evident. In the next chapter, an outline of future research in this direction is presented.

## REFERENCES

Acemoglu, D., and Robinson, J. A. (2018). The Narrow Corridor to Liberty: The Red Queen and the Struggle of State against Society. *Book manuscript.*

Franck, T.W. (2019, May 10). SEC approves the new Silicon Valley stock exchange backed by Marc Andreessen, other tech heavyweights. *Retrieved from https://www.cnbc.com/2019/05/10/sec-approves-new-silicon-valley-stock-exchange-backed-by-marc-andreessen-other-tech-heavyweights.html.*

Kumar, V., Venkatesan, R., Bohling, T., and Beckmann, D. (2008). Practice Prize Report—The power of CLV: Managing CLV at IBM. *Marketing Science*, *27*(4), 585-599.

Lin, K., Shyu, J., and Ding, K. (2017). A cross-strait comparison of innovation policy under industry 4.0 and sustainability development transition. *Sustainability*, 9(5), 786.

Mason, P. (2016). Postcapitalism: A guide to our future. *Macmillan.*

Mason, P. (2019). Clear Bright Future: A Radical Defence of the Human Being. *Penguin UK.*

Maresova, P., Soukal, I., Svobodova, L., Hedvicakova, M., Javanmardi, E., Selamat, A., and Krejcar, O. (2018). *Consequences of industry 4.0 in business and economics. Economies*, 6(3), 46.

Muñiz, M., Müller, E., and Kotak, P. (2019, September 16). An Innovation Agenda for Europe by Manuel Muñiz and Marietje Schaake. Retrieved from https://www.project-syndicate.org/commentary/europe-innovation-three-priorities-by-manuel-muniz-and-marietje-schaake-2019-09?utm_source=ProjectSyndicateNewsletterandutm_campaign=d866aab02d-contributor_newsletter_schaake_10_03_2020andutm_medium=emailandutm_term=0_73bad5b7d8-d866aab02d-105715273andmc_cid=d866aab02dandmc_eid=f6a22c60a9andbarrier=accesspaylog

Reischauer, G. (2018). Industry 4.0 as a policy-driven discourse to institutionalize innovation systems in manufacturing. *Technological Forecasting and Social Change*, 132, 26-33.

Stahl, H. K., Matzler, K., and Hinterhuber, H. H. (2003). Linking CLV with shareholder value. *Industrial Marketing Management*, *32*(4), 267-279.

Vinge, V. (1993, March). Technological singularity. In *VISION-21 Symposium sponsored by NASA Lewis Research Center and the Ohio Aerospace Institute* (pp. 30-31).

## KEY TERMS AND DEFINITIONS

**CLV:** Customer-lifetime value calculated by summing future cash flows that could be generated through the customer at hand. It is used primarily in startup valuations and decision-making models and inserts the customer's first philosophy.

**Shareholder's value:** Normally, profit maximization is the mantra that drives share price.

**Stakeholder's value:** Normally, societal benefits, environmental protection, and a healthy profit becomes the mantra.

**SDGs:** Coined by the United Nations to achieve sustainable development in 17 categories.